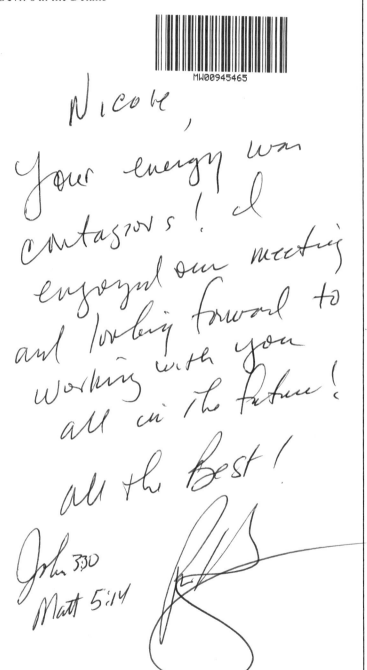

Nicole,

Your energy was contagious! I enjoyed our meeting and looking forward to working with you all in the future!

All the Best!

John 330
Matt 5:14

*"The Devil's In the Details"- Things that Challenge City
Government and the Language of Development*

Copyright @ 2018 by Rickey Hayes

Order additional copies of this book at Amazon.com or directly from
Retail Attractions, LLC, by email at office@retailattractions.com or
by phone at 918-376-6707.

This title is also available as an eBook from Amazon.com

the DEVIL'S in the DETAILS

Things that Challenge City Government and the Language of Development.

RICKEY HAYES

Author of **"City On A Hill- A Book About Cities And How To Make Them Better"**

DEDICATION #1: To My Family

When I look back over the six decades I have survived, my life has been through many different courses and has taken me down many different roads. There have been many blessings and many trials. But I have no complaints. The source of my life is the Lord of Lords and King of Kings who bore the cross and the nails for me. I have not always been the best example of a Christ follower, but His grace is sufficient for me. He will see me through. I trust him completely.

Speaking of blessings, let me thank my Creator once more for the loving parents who raised me and taught me when I was young. And let me thank Him again for Wendy Elizabeth Hayes, my loving bride of 38 years. Faithful and supportive, encouraging and wise, she has always been there through it all.

Then let me thank the four best people I know for what they have poured into their daddy's life. Dr. Ryan Elizabeth Parker, my firstborn daughter and one of the most amazing and hardworking physicians on the planet. Micah Paul Hayes, my first born son, who still works for me and with me every day at Retail Attractions. Micah is a traveler, can play anything with strings, and has sung his songs all over the world. I always loved music, just never could sit still long enough to learn anything but G, C, and D. Lauren Michelle Yoder, our third child and someone as gifted as anyone I've ever met, voice of an angel, and works hard every day making people beautiful. And then there is Joe Neil Hayes. A student at Baylor University, and one of the world's premier film makers and movie buffs. You will be reading about him one of these days. These are the most precious gifts that I have ever received and I love them dearly, and I am so very proud of each one of them.

Then there are five more little people that I can say actually have brought me much more joy than I deserve. Graham Edwin Parker, Collyn Elizabeth Parker, Hayes Elliot Parker, Charlotte Elizabeth Yoder, and Sullivan Morris Lynn Yoder. Those are the names on the birth certificates, here are their names when I'm around: Binky, Coco, Hank, Coots, and Sully. FYI grandchildren are the best blessings ever.

Thank you all for all you mean to me. I love you all more than words can reveal.

DEDICATION # 2: To My Friend Jim Shindler

One of the real reasons that Retail Attractions, LLC has been successful in our work with cities, counties, state governments, and a couple of sovereign nations (Choctaw Nations Business, Cherokee Nation) has been the simple fact that we have worked very hard to build and maintain quality relationships across the board. The foundation of any relationship is trust and confidence in the character of those in the relationship. Retail development is a relationship based business. The people you work with affect your company, and your company affects and influences the people you work with. The relationships you nurture and maintain are very important to the future quality of the mutual work you are able to accomplish. I first met Jim Shindler when he was the head of development for Dallas based Hunt Properties. I knew when I first met him that he was focused and driven, had a mile-long resume of world-class retail product in several states, and that he loved and adored his wife and two children. When I met him I knew very little at all about retail development. After a few hours in the car with him on a site selection tour of the city I worked for, I marveled at his vision and what he explained to me to be the potential of what could happen in our little town. I will have to say at this point I did not know if we could pull off what he was seeing, but over the next six years everything he shared with me on the date of that first meeting came to pass. Jim developed three phases of national retail and restaurant tenants in a town so small that the majority of the retailers who ended up in that initial lineup told me they had never opened in a market as small as ours. Nearly two decades later the retail is still churning out premium sales, and has created millions and millions of dollars in sales tax revenue. Since then I have worked with Jim on many other projects and he is one of the best friends I have, and in fact it was Jim who really opened the door for me to start my company. I will be forever grateful for his advice and the support and encouragement he has shown to me over the years. Jim has his own company now and operates it (Conifer Real Estate, Inc.) out of Southlake, Texas.

Jim, thanks for all you have done for me over the years. I appreciate you more than you know. I'm not ready to retire, so let's do some more.

RH

DEDICATION # 3: To Michael Ray Nunneley

I have had the privilege of meeting many city managers, hundreds in fact, in cities large and small all over this country. Being a city manager is without a doubt one of the most difficult jobs ever, especially if you do it right. Some managers manage their communities and their elected officials well, and some managers get managed by their elected officials. Imagine working in an environment where you knew more about what needed to be done because of your training and experience, and yet five or more people, none of which knew a fraction of what needed to happen in any given situation, are all trying to tell you what to do and threatening to fire you if you didn't get their personal goals done. When a city has a real manager, who knows his stuff, and how to challenge his staff and pull work out of them that they didn't know they could do, magic happens in the community. I have experienced that myself and it is a very rewarding career choice. If your town is managed by an ego driven bully, it's a place that grinds you to powder. Even worse is when an unstable city council makes the manager's life miserable and he becomes their slave, without a mind of his own. That's messed up and produces nothing but chaos and confusion.

I had the privilege and honor of working with one of the best city managers in the world over the past six years. Michael Ray Nunneley, was one of the most gifted, genuine, and salt-of-the-earth human beings I have ever met. His experience was honed in small Oklahoma towns for nearly four decades. Mannford, Oklahoma, just a few minutes west of downtown Tulsa, is a beautiful town sitting on a hill over one of Oklahoma's many pristine bodies of water, Keystone Lake. Mannford was blessed to have Mike Nunneley as their manager, and the community is one of the most financially set cities in the country because of his vision and talents to run the community like the multimillion dollar corporation that it is. The city owns its own water, sanitary sewer, natural gas, and electric utilities. A few years back when natural gas prices skyrocketed, the towns in Oklahoma who had to get their natural gas through the big gas franchise companies were in a tizzy because of the outrageous prices. Mannford citizen's natural gas prices went down, because Mike had bought and stored a whole winters worth of natural gas because he had seen the price jump coming a year or two before.

Mike's entrepreneurial skills were not his best asset to many of us who looked up to him. Mike took me under his wings and

9

singlehandedly guided me through the first two years I was in business for myself, even through the recession of 2008-2009 when I thought I was going to starve to death. He opened doors for me to help many other Oklahoma communities, and that was and still is a huge blessing for me. He also raised some of the best tomatoes in the world on the good soil of his Mannford garden. He told me the best thing God ever did for the human race was to create the "homegrown" tomato.

Mike passed away the week this book was finished after complications from cancer treatment. I loved him because he treated me like I was his son. He taught me, made me laugh, and gave me some of the soundest advice I believe I ever heard. He said to me more than once that when you get so busy you can't think straight, shut down and go fishing.

Mike, I dedicate this book to you, and to those whose lives you touched like you touched mine.

Rickey Hayes
May 24, 2018

Forward

I've known and worked with Rickey Hayes for over twenty years and was only a few minutes into Rickey's chapter on "Are We There Yet?" when I knew he had a winner in this book. I have been involved in economic development efforts for over thirty years and have not seen anything that has captured the essence of the frustrations and feelings of euphoric success that accompany retail economic projects like this book has accomplished. It should be required reading for all municipal officials from Florida to Washington state.

Rickey has succeeded in putting together both a basic primer and a deep reality in one writing. Whether you are a newly elected official or a staff member on a municipal/county team this is a powerful compilation of realities and strategy "Are We There Yet?" truths he so ardently communicated and had the old feelings of angst that accompanied the chapter on "Tension". Rickey has captured the reality of economic development so well that it demands your attention.

It should be noted by the reader, that my initial introduction to Rickey was for the purpose of discussing an employment opportunity for him with the City of Owasso. Though that specific opportunity did not materialize (when it became obvious that the particular job we were offering, and Rickey's obvious strengths did not match), I did see in him a natural talent for communication and a skill set that would make him an asset to the City's Economic Development Team. Working with Rickey over a period of seven years resulted in both of us becoming attuned to the keys that contribute to the success of our community's retail development program. While he had no economic development experience when we met him, Rickey "plunged" into the efforts with an enthusiasm that was foundational to his learning and ultimately to the success of our community literally becoming a retail marketplace that attracted more than 65% of its consumers from outside our city. Now, his experience and passion for helping cities is being utilized across the country to create local economic environments that encourage investment and growth in the retail sectors of those communities he serves.

I was impressed with how successful Rickey was in clearly communicating, via the pages of this book, the idea of how important each player is in a successful development strategy. After reading this soon to be classic, it becomes obvious that a successful economic development strategy requires the cooperative effort of the "village". Fire chiefs, Public Works staffers, Planners, Inspectors, Councilors, Commissioners, the Chambers of Commerce (and all who want a better economic environment for their community and children) should pick up this book and study the contrasting primer and country philosophy contained herein.

Rodney J Ray
May 24, 2018

The Devil's in the Details

TABLE CONTENTS

ENDORSEMENTS

On January 31, 2011, I retired as the Deputy Chief of Police for the Broken Arrow Police Department. On February 1, 2011, I began the next chapter of my professional life as the Economic Development Coordinator for the City of Broken Arrow. Rickey Hayes was a speaker at one of the first economic development training sessions I attended. During the presentation, I learned we had something in common; both of us went from law enforcement to economic development. Over the next seven years, I have never missed an opportunity to spend time with Rickey and pick his brain on all aspects of my new career. In airports, airplanes, in restaurants and conferences, Rickey has always taken the time to mentor me, answer my questions, and provide valuable information to help me be successful and improve the quality of life for the citizens of the City of Broken Arrow. Frankly, if Rickey charged for all of the help he has provided me, I could not afford to pay. I have a signed copy of his first book, and I am looking forward to reading the next one.

Norman Stephens, Economic Development Coordinator / Assistant to the City Manager City of Broken Arrow, Oklahoma

I guess fate led me to Rickey Hayes. I discovered him through his first book, '*City On A Hill- A Book About Cities And How To Make Them Better*'. I purchased his book online and read with great interest his writings about growing communities and retail development from the public sector side. Then, out of the blue, our city lost one of its primary general retail sources and the book took on a whole new relevance. I called him one day, he was traveling to another city, and as we talked for an extended time, I felt connected to his expertise, his openness to share with us, and felt like his company might be able to help us.

When we experienced our setback in the retail sector, the loss of our Walmart store, Rickey and the Retail Attractions team were the right fit for us. Retail Attractions quickly educated our team and our community on the ins and outs of how "retail" works. They quickly gave us a better understanding of what, realistically, our community was capable of achieving given our size and location. Rickey and his team's approach was very hands-on, relationship based, and founded on local market data. Their team worked with us to create "our" retail strategy moving forward.

Once Rickey and the Retail Attractions team visited and got to know our community, they became much more than a consultant. They became part of our team and were personally vested in our success. Knowing that they are a champion for our community is very reassuring.

Rickey and his team understands economic development and that larger understanding is very helpful to us. Rickey and Retail Attraction's professional, but approachable, style, their experience, their understanding of public and private stakeholders, and their ability to connect is why we are confident in our selection.

I would highly recommend Retail Attractions, LLC and Rickey Hayes to any community new to the retail environment or facing retail challenges.

Michael Pavey
Mayor
City of Rushville, Indiana

For anyone who has worked in local government for any length of time, we know that there are many tools available to regulate things like development, property maintenance, nuisances, etc. However, when comes to encouraging and incentivizing economic development we sometimes rely on too few tools and have too narrow of a vision. As a city administrator who was looking to hire a commercial/retail development consultant I happened to have a chance to meet Rickey Hayes of Retail Attractions. It didn't take long for me to realize that Rickey didn't just talk the language of retail and commercial development, but he actually knew it. Since that time Rickey has confirmed what I have always believed, that many development deals are based more on relationships than just numbers, that the quality of life within a community matters just as much as the economic demographics, and that a successful economic development strategy requires a comprehensive set of tools, a broad vision and telling of a good story. Rickey has helped our community achieve success in developing a strategy and telling our story. I can't wait to read his new book.

Phillip Patterson, City Manager
Siloam Springs, Arkansas

Our community had a habit of "letting" things happen instead of "making" things happen. We made a conscious effort a few years ago to step up and be more aggressive in our retail recruitment. Hiring Rickey Hayes and his firm Retail Attractions was one of the smartest things we have done. His contacts throughout the retail world are invaluable for a community like ours. The evidence that he knows what he is doing is on sites all over Enid, Oklahoma.

Brent Kisling
Enid Regional Development Alliance

PREFACE

I said to myself when I finished the manuscript for my first book that I was glad to get done and that I never wanted to do that again. I never aspired to be a writer and if you have read the first book *"City on a Hill- a Book about Cities and How to Make Them Better"*, (available right now for purchase on Amazon.com or at www.retailattractions.com) you may say to yourself that I am definitely not a writer. If you said that I would probably agree with you. I'm certainly not a good one. However, I fancy myself as a guy that has to say something when he sees the ignorant, uninformed, or chronically mistaken making decisions that affect not only their city, but their own or their family's quality of life for future generations. Sometimes I don't want to say something, but most of the time I can't help myself.

My work, my job, my chosen profession is to help communities improve their quality of life, their revenue streams, and their economic development strategies and goals. I have been doing work in this field for over 17 years. I have worked for the public sector for over 30 years.

The public sector does a lot of things well. The public sector provides essential basic services to their constituents. Good services like good drinking water, sanitary sewer services that allow toilets to flush, streets that we can traverse in our automobiles without damaging our tires or our bodies. The public sector provides law enforcement services to protect and serve, other public safety services like fire protection and ambulance services. The public sector provides recreational opportunities, like sports parks and walking trails so that we can stay healthy and dog parks for our pets to enjoy. The public sector, and I am talking about those who manage our cities, who work tirelessly in public service, and those elected officials (city councilors, city commissioners, city and county trustees, etc.) who are in charge of our tax dollars and all other sources of public money and how it is spent, these people have tremendous responsibilities.

Most of the time those elected to represent the citizens in a town or city, have no experience in street engineering, construction, or maintenance. Most of the time they have never treated drinking water to insure our water is pure and free of all impurities and is safe to drink. I promise you that most elected officials have no working knowledge of hydrology and how to contain storm water runoff so as not to flood our homes. Most city councilors don't have any idea how to extract an injured person from a wrecked automobile, provide basic first aid at the scene, and how to safely get that unfortunate soul to a hospital in the fastest way. Most city commissioners have never had to face a desperate drug addict who is burglarizing a house in your neighborhood, or talk down a mentally ill homeless man who is having a schizophrenic episode on a street corner at two in the morning while the rest of us sleep peacefully in our warm beds. Yet we put them (our elected officials) in a position to make decisions to use public money to fund these services, and give them the authority to make decisions that will affect ours or our children or grandchildren's lives for decades to come.

Now I said all that to tell you that something as important as economic development, which is the foundational public sector vehicle for funding the future, is in the hands of people who probably have no idea or even a basic understanding of the specialized work and processes that need to be in place before the city can even stand a chance of success in this endeavor.

Yes, it is serious business. All economic development is a process. There are predictable outcomes to each step. All parts of the process need to be engaged, if one is missed or neglected, you can't just say "Oh well, we forgot that part." And all successful economic development will cause change, which is in itself hard to manage, especially in the public sector setting. And all economic development is at its foundation very holistic. There is the job creation element. There is the residential development element. There is the retail element. There is also the need to support the local educational (public / private school, community college, tech center, university) system, to have good and ready access to the delivery of medical care, and again the delivery and maintenance of foundational city services.

It's complicated. And it requires some level of experienced, qualified, and professional personnel. That is why good city managers make the big bucks. Because the elected officials usually have no experience or qualifications for these specific duties, the need for professional administrators is growing each year. The elected officials in Owasso, Oklahoma when I was hired consisted of a plant worker, a truck driver, an owner of a hardware store, a computer programmer, and a guy who worked for a heat exchanger manufacturer. These folks were in place when about a billion dollars' worth of retail growth blew the doors off our community. But we had a talented city manager and a dedicated and hardworking city staff. And we survived. And I will always be convinced that the reason we survived is that the one goal the city manager instilled in all of us was that economic development was the core reason any of us had a job.

I felt like I had to write this book to address a couple or three glaring problems and issues that I have seen destroy foundational economic development efforts in a bunch of cities. These monsters are found in every community, even though they do all they can to destroy, sometimes cities are able survive them. But left unaddressed, believe me they will always be lying in wait, just under the surface, and if not dealt with and understood they will cause people to get fired, get voted out of office, or worse yet become passive and simply walk away with bitter anger seething in the hearts of the good people who have tried to make the place they live better.

With the advent of social media these destroyers of momentum have been fortified to do more damage. With Facebook, Twitter, Instagram, etc., any misguided wing-nut can twist, pervert, and demolish the truth. And they can do their evil deeds from the comfort of their own home, and many times they can remain anonymous. Ignorance is a disease, and is not curable in most cases. Rarely will an ignorant person admit they are ignorant and accept the wisdom and the vision of the ones that are called to public service. And, yes, I will admit that sometimes the ignorant ones are on the public sector team.

What are these issues that have the power to destroy the momentum of positive growth and change in a community?

Politics and not grasping the amount of time it takes to get through the process of change, and disclosing things before they mature. Not all politics are bad, but you will agree with me that most modern political rhetoric is nauseating and frustrating. What we need is leaders. Visionary leaders, humble, transparent, and courageous leaders. Truth tellers who live in the real world. Not corrupt deceivers, not greedy ego maniacs. Do these people exist? Of course. I have had the privilege of meeting literally hundreds of these folks. Both on the administrative and the political side of city government. I have also met some real nasty, slimy, and sinister city folks. On the other hand the private sector has the same demographics; there are some of the best people in the world doing development business in the marketplace and some real monsters and crooks as well. So politics can cure problems and kill at the same time. Another big monster is the amount of time it takes to see these development projects completed. It takes a LONG time. Many times a retail deal will take so much time that council seats and city managers both change during the scope of time the deal takes.

Every time I orient a new city client I spend a major amount of time talking about these two big monsters, and a side issue of the importance of confidentiality. There is much to say about how, when, and where to go public with news of a new deal. Between social media and newspapers stirring things up, awful things can happen. At the end of the day, all we have left to do is keep working.

So the first four chapters of this book are about the big monsters that keep the public sector side of economic development in turmoil and the final chapter is a lexicon of development terminology for public sector personnel.

A vision of what could be, consensus, and everybody pulling in the same direction can certainly improve the quality of life in every city in the world. Our company believes that we are called to assist communities in doing that very thing.

We would love to assist your community. Experience is worth a lot, because experience does two things, it lets you know what works and more importantly it lets you know what doesn't work. If you know a city manager or city councilor, or a city staffer at any level in your town, buy this book for them. It will help create opportunity for change. Healthy things grow, and growing things change. And every change that improves the quality of life in your city is a good thing.

CHAPTER 1
TENSION
[OR THINGS THAT SLOW DEVELOPMENT FROM THE INSIDE]

Many terms that are associated with economic development are hard to define in nice, neat and concise language. Many would not think that the word 'tension' could be regularly applied to the process of economic development, but those in the arena daily know for sure that tension in our chosen field of effort is an everyday fact of life. We all know tension. We have all experienced it. The world around us is filled with tension. We have tension in our homes, our schools, and especially in government at all levels. Tension is described in many ways. Tension is what we have when opposing elements or philosophies clash. Tension is created when a state or condition of mental, emotional, philosophical, or other opposing conditions collide. Tension occurs when the physical or metaphysical condition of people is being stretched or strained. Economic development brings change. All change causes tension. And since change is inevitable, so is tension and the pressure it brings.

We all are aware that healthy things grow. Healthy people grow, healthy plants grow, and healthy animals grow. Healthy businesses grow. Healthy cities grow. Growth brings change. Think about it. Growth makes everything change. Change brings tension. Tension brings challenges. Naturally challenges produce more tension. Since tension and tribulations are a fact of life, we need to not only accept that tension is a part of everyday work and life, but learn to bear it and to work through it and find creative ways to overcome the stigma and effects of it. Change brings with it the need to build consensus among those involved, because many times the tension of change pulls people apart.

All of life is inter-relational. Economic development is a relationship based process. When city leaders seek to improve the quality of life of the citizens, or when they seek to develop and build revenue streams to meet the growing expenses of providing essential services to citizens, tension will arise. Everybody has an opinion of what needs to be done. Elected officials and city administrators live in a tension filled environment. Relationships get strained, egos get wounded, and tension builds, sometimes to the point of anger, serious discord, and broken relationships. They don't have college courses in business school that teach how to stay in relationship when everybody disagrees with you.

What is even more frightening is that in the decade that our company has been in the business of assisting cities with retail recruiting and economic development consulting, the state of retail growth and really the whole retail industry has been in a constant state of tension and change. The effect of online versus brick and mortar sales, iconic retailers closing, retailers and restaurants declaring bankruptcy, and poor sales has been the focus for many discussions by both retail tenants and the developers who build for them. These changes create lots of issues for cities, especially in the smaller, more rural markets. Retail changes are occurring rapidly, sometimes even day to day.

When you work with cities every day like our firm does, many times one of the first things you notice is the obvious level of tension in the conversations. City managers are tense, city councilors and other elected officials are tense, city employees are tense. When stress and tension are evident many times these people who are responsible for making the decisions are very reluctant to pull the trigger on anything that might get them in trouble with their bosses, or the public. Even when the choices they are making are needed in order to cause something or some process or some element of city, county, state, or federal government to change for the better tension rises. Almost every decision in any government setting is

Almost every decision in any government setting is going to make somebody angry.

going to make somebody angry. I said in a speech one time to a couple hundred city stakeholders that the mayor of that particular city had a tough job. He was having to make decisions so that things in the community that had been stagnant for many years could change, and many of the controversial decisions he was making were directly causing the overall quality of life in that community to improve almost immediately. I said being the mayor there was like being a fire hydrant in a town with a lot of dogs. If there was a fire that the mayor was going to be a hero, but every day when he went to work he was going to get sprayed by every citizen that walked by. I do not know if you have ever been verbally urinated on by angry (pissed off) people, but I am pretty sure that it is not fun.

Economic development is a topic that is being discussed by every community in the country every day. It matters not what population, what amenities, what financial benefits a particular city is blessed with. Good city administrators are looking for ways to increase revenue, improve relationships, and improve the quality of life in their particular town. Every community that is healthy is in some stage of growth. Communities that are not growing, or that have slim chances of growth are in trouble. The revenue demands of non-growth cities are growing even though the community may not be. That is not a healthy situation. Tensions are increasing. Decisions have to be made. This is the environment where our company works. In terms of job security, we have a fertile field in which to labor.

Any proposed new development and / or any change to the status quo brings to light issues that cause tension in a progressive local municipality. Let's look at a few examples. As I have stated, one of the many things our company does for cities is direct recruiting of retail and restaurants. There are several foundational elements to this work, and even though it is fairly complex, there are some basic tools that we use. We look at each client community's demographic and market data, we examine the national level retailers that are in the market already, and we look at the availability of developable real estate. We also analyze the leakage or opportunity gaps in the local market and help local governments plug the holes by recruiting retail goods and services that are missing in the market.

Many times when word gets out that the city has contracted with a consulting group to recruit new national level retailers, local mom and pop business owners and other well-meaning people in the community will develop concerns and phobias that we are trying to "ruin" their business. Nothing could be further from the truth. In fact, in all the many years I have been in this line of work, and the multiple millions of square feet of new retail and restaurant tenants we have helped facilitate in over 440 cities in 39 states, I have witnessed time after time that the addition of new national retail in every city, even in small communities, raises the bar and increases sales in the local setting. What happens is that many consumers in the market will begin to shop local, and stay in town rather than leave to spend their money elsewhere. And consumers outside the local setting will come into the market to enjoy the new retail offerings. This phenomena usually produces sales growth for the locally owned retailers and restaurants in small and rural markets.

Let me give you a real world example of what this looks like. A city I worked in had a national building materials retailer (Lowe's) that was doing well, had a great location, and was drawing consumers from outside of the local retail market. They had been open for several years without any real competition. Another national building materials retailer (Home Depot) contacted me and wanted to enter the market. They picked a site, put a contract on a local tract of real estate, and then asked me if the city would consider incentivizing them to come. There were a few development issues such as a sanitary sewer extension, and some fairly intensive road and access issues. The cost of the added development issues was around $1.25

million. Now if you put yourself in my position, this issue appeared to be problematic. We (the city) already had a premium national brand that was doing over $40 million in sales annually. Now we had a competing retailer wanting in the market and asking the city for some public funds for an incentive to offset some of their development costs.

My fear and concern was that if I asked the city council to consider providing incentives to the retailer, and we put public funds in the deal, that when the retailer opened we were going to cannibalize the sales of the existing retailer. Now please understand, when new retail comes to any market it is very possible that sales numbers from same category retailers may change. As I discussed the deal with the city manager and staff, and we began to educate the city council on the request for incentives, concern arose and I was charged with the responsibility to do more research and to see what I could find out from the retailer and from communities that had seen the same or similar issues.

I started the due diligence with Home Depot and what I learned from the corporate real estate person was that the retailer believed that Lowe's was only capturing limited market sales. I will never forget the statement that the real estate representative declared… "they (Lowe's) are just scratching the surface of the market". The next statement was even more shocking. She said she was pretty sure that if we could help Home Depot get into the market, that Lowe's sales would go up. I spoke with a few city staffers from other communities that had seen both retailers come to town, and the information that they provided was inconclusive.

After much discussion, the city council took a stand that if a retailer wanted into the city, they were going to try to always say yes. So we put together a development agreement, incentivized the deal with new sales tax created by the new store, and waited patiently for Home Depot to open. And open they did! After the initial 12 months of sales we anxiously compared sales data from both retailers. Their first year sales were just under $40 million. Guess what Lowe's did in the same twelve month period? Their sales increased over the previous year from around $40 million to just over $47 million. So the moral to the story is that home improvement sales doubled from $40 million to over $80 million annually and all we did was add a competitive retailer.

I have also seen this happen on a smaller scale when national quick serve restaurants have entered much smaller markets and added a couple million in sales, with the existing restaurants in the market going up as well.

Competition in almost every category is good. But sometimes it adds tension and maybe some tribulations and trials in the local community. Tension and trials are stressful but a necessary part of change.

One of the other areas of origin for stress, tension, and tribulations is in local politics. I could tell you stories that are almost inconceivable and unbelievable to rational human beings. Having worked in over 440 cities, I have seen and heard some local political banter. Believe me. Why any sane individual would ever want to go to work as a city manager is beyond me. But people do. And I have met some of the finest

Change is the common denominator of all things that are healthy and growing.

men and women on the planet in this role of city administrator. But for every good one I have met, there are others that should never be allowed to run anything, let alone a city. The good managers all have some common traits. For starters, good city managers are vision casters. They see the Promised Land. They have been to the top of the mountain, looked over the landscape, and see what changes have to take place to get where they need to go. Notice the word change. Good city managers are change agents. Good managers are not scared to pull the trigger on change. Change is the common denominator of all things that are healthy and growing. The problem is that almost every component of life resists change. We like ruts. We like familiarity. People like routine and status quo. Especially in the public arena.

The most common city government scenario you encounter is the council / manager form of government. This type of city government is overseen by a number of elected city councilors who hire a city manager to run the day to day administration of the city. There are other government arrangements, such as strong mayor / council. In this setting the mayor is elected to oversee the affairs and business of the city, and works with an elected council. Many times the mayor and council will hire an administrator to take care of the duties of city government while they (the mayor and council) set policy and procedural direction for the community. Some towns have an aldermanic form of government, where aldermen / trustees are elected to oversee the political and administrative affairs of the city. Sometimes the trustees / commissioners will hire an administrator to oversee city departments. Whatever the type of government, there are people involved. And as you guessed already, some people do not see eye to eye.

Each type of political system has advantages and disadvantages, but the common thread is that in most instances some individual is responsible for making decisions that affect the direction the community takes, the pace of change, and the sometimes overwhelming job of building and maintaining political consensus. That is where the tension comes in.

City councilors are usually elected for a two or three year term, and many times city managers get their walking papers in two to three years. With the city manager or lead administrator comes the implied responsibility of setting vision. With council seats potentially changing with every election, and managers getting fired all the time, no vision can get planted. A very wise man once said, "Without a vision, the people perish". As you can imagine, in a visionless city nothing is ever going to change. Remember healthy things grow, and growing things change. All change is either positive or negative. Nothing stays the same. And there is no middle ground where problems and issues can

Growing cities require great leaders at the helm.

get placed in time out. Twenty years ago the average tenure for a city manager in Oklahoma was around two years and a month or two. Today that number has improved a little, but it is still less than five years. That causes tension. Imagine a career path where you knew you had to look for another job every few years. Imagine with me for a second what it would be like to have a job where you had five bosses, and all it takes to get you fired is for three of your five bosses to have a bad day at the same time. It's scary. You have to be tough to be a city manager.

Good city managers must be a literal 'jack of all trades". Growing cities require great leaders at the helm. The job description of a city administrator comes with tons of responsibility, requires a tremendous amount of courage, and for growing cities, or cities that want to grow, the manager has to be able to bring consensus out of chaos. Time after time. City managers work long hours, endure more meetings than you can even imagine, and deal with angry people every day.

In municipal government sometimes issues come along that require immediate attention. These unannounced problems may require large amounts of public revenues to address the issue. Or even worse they may be issues mandated by the state or federal government, with no federal or state money to help pay the costs. Imagine having to deal with five bosses, staff, and the public, the press, and social media and attempting to fix problems. City managers do it every day.

Sometimes the unfortunate issues in the city aren't able to be addressed because the city manager's bosses (the city council) are actually the issue. I probably have met, spoken with, presented to, tried to persuade, and have been frustrated with more city councilors than you could imagine. I have marveled at the humility and leadership that I have seen from some elected officials. But I have also seen some of the most ignorant, crass, and twisted individuals I have ever met in a council seat. When you combine unity and consensus, with humble and wise men and women, who want to serve their city only because they feel called to the duty with a higher calling, and who simply desire to see their community be the best that it can be, the quality of life in that town is going to be rising constantly. On the other hand, when elected officials are only there to further personal agendas, or when the reason for even running for council was to fire somebody, or some other kooky reason instead of a simple desire to make their city the best city it could be, nothing good happens.

With the advent and growth of social media, communities are able to educate, survey, communicate, and listen to their citizens now, more than ever before. Social media can also be the instigator of fake news, falsehoods, and fairy tales that can keep the political goings on in a community completely in a chaotic storm for months at a time. I am not saying that cities should not use all available means (including social media) to educate, communicate, and inform their people. The problem is when you enter the world of social media, every word that's spoken, every video that's posted, anything and everything is broadcast to the public. Because it's broadcast to the public, and shared online, it needs to be monitored closely. When communities use the internet and social media to communicate public information, announcements, and any other thing they post, they are at that time, asking for a response. I do not mean literally asking for a response, but in a very tangible way they should expect public comments. Cutting edge cities (and cities that want to be) should respond promptly and properly to those public comments. Not responding, or waiting too long to respond causes all hell to break loose. Even worse, an improper response causes people to be angry, or get fired, or voted out of office. If you are going to get in public service, or if you are even considering running for city council one day, you should know that you can literally change lives for the better, and make your city and the people who choose to live there a much better place. However, if you have these same thoughts and you are not emotionally stable and mature, let it go. There are other places to volunteer and other places to work. Believe me, you wouldn't like it in the public arena anyway.

Recently one of my client communities ran into a storm regarding an election. This particular city has made some changes in policy over the last couple of years that have been part of a foundational change in strategy that has moved the historic Oklahoma town out of the past into the real world. Efforts have been made to bring the old and outdated ways of local government to a more modern, more transparent, more accessible, and more efficient way of doing things. Code enforcement, land use planning and a strategic zoning and economic development planning has been instituted and has already prompted new private sector investment. New retail has been added, and a manufacturing company just located in the community, creating new jobs. New jobs are always good news in any city. In an effort to modernize and create a more efficient system of day to day operations in the local municipal setting the city council wanted to create a change in the way three key city positions were employed. Under current local laws, the police chief, the city treasurer, and the city clerk are elected instead of hired by the city council. There was no job descriptions, no educational requirements, no experience necessary, no certifications and training required, etc. for any of these positions. So an election was called to ask the public to vote to change the archaic codes and allow the city council to appoint these three positions in an effort to insure that in the future these administrative offices would be staffed by trained, competent, and accountable people. The current police chief, city treasurer, and city clerk all supported this change unanimously. However when the election was called the local social media exploded with a tsunami of false and inaccurate posts, and attacks on the mayor and other city employees that literally accused the mayor of sinister and perhaps criminal acts. The city tried to answer the false and misleading sewer on social media and other means but the CAVE people (Citizens Against Virtually Everything) were not interested in the least in knowing the truth and the benefits of the change, their minds were so set on resisting all change, even beneficial change that would have made the city better immediately and would have allowed positive change to continue long into the future. Those who said this whole thing was a power grab by the mayor, and that the mayor was taking away their right to vote, were obviously forgetting the key truth. The same city council that they elected by a vote of the citizens themselves thought it was the absolute best thing to do. The vote was overwhelming to resist positive, more efficient government, and more local control by opposing change at all costs. Even change that would have made the city better for years to come.

People soon forget that quality of life is not something that is stable. Change only comes in one of two forms. It is either positive and will make things better, or when folks resist positive change, they should remember that change is still going to come. And change is always dynamic. It always makes things better or worse. Refusing to change is saying we like it like it is. The heart breaker is that "it" won't stay like it is, "it" will begin to decline. Look at nature, if you think this principle is not true. Yards without constant maintenance become weed beds, young strong bodies without constant maintenance become fat, weak bodies. The same principle works in cities. Remember the ONLY constant thing in life is change. Positive change makes things better, negative change or resisting positive change always is going to make things worse. Truth is not always calming and comforting. Sometimes truth is a howling wind that people don't want to face. People who believe that things will stay like they are and that the way things are is better than the way things could be are very short sighted and are simply ignorant of reality. Nothing stays the way it is. It either grows or it declines. There is no magic middle ground. If you are not continually improving, then what you are doing is merely maintenance. And once you start maintenance, you will never be able to stay ahead of the decline. You might be able to slow the declination, but you can't avoid it. The only way to stay ahead is to be in the mood of constantly improving every facet of public life and the municipal process.

The extent of how far political bullying will go is shocking. I have seen some unbelievable behavior from supposedly civilized people firsthand and heard of many more political horror stories. I know of situations where economic development efforts in a community were met with threats of shaming, organized boycotts, even physical bullying and intimidation.

I have a lot more horror stories I could tell you. In many years of working for public entities (from both the public side and from the private sector side as well), I am convinced that city politics and politics in general are a necessary evil. But let me assure you that instability of any kind in the public sector certainly will delay and most assuredly impede, and can even kill any positive economic development deal. It is indeed rare to find a community that has a visionary city manager, a council of elected officials that are unified and totally supportive of the city manager, and a staff of committed public servants carrying out the vision of positive growth. I have worked in over 440 cities in 39 states and I can honestly say that I have witnessed only a handful of communities across this country that are serious and committed to building consensus, and managing the constant call to improve the quality of life of their citizens. This is not to say that there aren't hundreds of communities with the desire to work toward the idea. But alas, bad mojo, ego, pride, ignorance, lies, greed, lust for control and power, and basic incompetence are eating the town from the inside like a cancer. If the private sector even gets a scent of political infighting and instability, they get spooked. This many times can cause delays, and anyone who has worked in economic development work knows the adage "time kills deals".

I am always looking for the leader in a city. Who is the influencer? Who is the person that "pulls the trigger"? Where is the team? What is the vision? Is the vision practical? Where is the consensus? Where is the desire for forward momentum and change? Many times what I see is infighting, backstabbing, ignorance, CAVE people, NIMBYs, and dirty politics. Translated: CAVE people are Constantly Against Virtually Everything. NIMBYs are people who are ok with change but Not In My Back Yard. If you want to see dirty politics turn on cable television or talk radio or look at social media. It's not hard to recognize.

If your city politics are dirty and there is a lot of public fighting going on I implore every man, woman, and child to not stand by and watch. Take a step, get involved, and become a peacemaker and a consensus builder. If your elected officials and city staff are the good guys and they are trying to change your community for the better, go support them every way you can. If your city administrators and elected officials are the problem, go on the offensive and start change with getting these knuckleheads in other lines of work. Vote, speak up, and yes, attend public meetings. Margaret Mead's statement made many years ago is still true today. She said **"Never doubt that a small group of thoughtful, committed citizens can change the world; indeed, it's the only thing that ever has."**

What hinders growth and positive change in cities? Bad politics, ignorance, apathy, corruption, lies, un-kept promises, passivity, lack of vision, inflated egos, disunity, and greed. It shouldn't be government versus citizens and citizens versus government. It should be citizens who love their community and want to see and embrace growth and change, active in local politics, supporting and standing with those who have been placed in the place of leadership by the citizens they represent, all working toward the same goal and all pulling in the same direction to make their community the best it can be.

CHAPTER 2

ARE WE THERE YET?

One of the questions asked of our company in every new city is how long will it be before we can see the fruits of your labor, or a return on our investment of public funding. That is a reasonable and perfectly understandable question. The answer is almost always troubling to elected officials because the truth is that all development takes longer than everybody involved thinks it will. The process of economic development is painfully slow. Always has been, and always will be. Retail development (or any other type of development) is slow because there is so much risk and so many different personalities and egos involved. It's also a long and grinding process because nearly every step of development has a large variety of moving parts and puzzle pieces. The retail industry as a whole is trying to figure out what the future holds while retail consumers are bombarded with opportunities to purchase. Not only in stand-alone brick and mortar buildings, malls, power centers, lifestyle centers, mixed-use centers, outlet centers but also at work on their computers, or from their smart phone in the middle of a traffic jam. Online sales are off the scale, and consumers can buy literally anything they desire, and have it delivered direct to their home in a few hours, many times with free shipping.

Even when retail made sense, it still took years to get projects done. I have witnessed small QSR (quick serve restaurants) deals that once the site was entitled got built in 120-150 days. I have also witnessed first-hand stand-alone single tenant retail deals take multiple years. While I was the director of Owasso, Oklahoma economic development the city manager and I drove to northwest Arkansas and had a meeting with a developer about Sam's Club interest in our retail market. The meeting went well and we left that day knowing several things we did not know when we went. Sam's was indeed interested. We had a site, a qualified, experienced developer, and a city council that saw the value in new retail development. What we did not know was that it would ultimately take seven full years before the store opened for business. Although the original intent of all involved never wavered, the circumstances surrounding the development changed constantly over the next seven years. First the private landowner had a bout with cancer. The real estate methodology and philosophy of the retailer changed dramatically. City administration changed and took a whole different attitude to commercial development. City infrastructure had to be taken under a US highway and there were issues with storm water and then a home owners association at an upscale residential development in the same neighborhood as the commercial development organized and lawyered up to fight the development. Keep in mind the original intent of the retailer to open a new unit in our city never changed. But issue after issue came up and resistance arose that required multiple public meetings and lots of politicking to address. I am happy to say that even though the development of this project took seven long years to build, it eventually got done and the anchor tenant is now on a site that is completely urbanized and every square inch of potential development real estate on the corner is covered with sales tax producing national and regional retail and restaurant tenants.

I have said before and I will say it here

again, the very toughest task I face when our company gets hired by a public sector entity is educating the elected officials and sometimes the city manager and staff on just how long this process takes. It is absolutely the most frustrating facet of my job. I can show them by experience what happens, show them the timeline, teach about all the myriad of issues that cause delays, point out the city's own bureaucratic development restrictions and codes that eat up time, point out possible economic

Have you ever seen anything involving any government body at any level move quickly?

trends that can delay development, explain environmental and site issues (like my favorite bug, the American Burying Beatle) that can slow down the project, even point to federal storm water issues that are common on development sites where the local civil engineers have to collaborate with the Corps of Engineers from the federal government, and still they ask…. "Why does it take so long?" Let me ask you this simple question. Have you ever seen anything involving any government body at any level move quickly?

We all know the answer to that.

I came to a Tulsa, Oklahoma suburb in the summer of 2001 to interview for the chief of police position in the growing city of Owasso. Through the interview process, I made a connection with the city manager and several of the city staff and in the course of the interview process, through a mutual decision not to take the law enforcement job, I did end up accepting the job of directing the economic development efforts of the city. I started on the first day of July in this position and worked very hard for the first year and produced not one tangible thing. After a very frustrating few months I was beginning to wonder why I moved my family to Oklahoma from Texas. Sometime near the end of my first year in Owasso, I started digging into the operations of four retailers, in fact the only four retailers that our city had already operating in our market. Three of the four retailers were all national brands, very recognizable national brands, and the fourth retailer was our grocery retailer, which was a regional family owned brand, called Reasor's Foods. The three other national brands consisted of a big Walmart Super Center, Kohls, and Lowe's Home Improvement.

Besides Reasor's, the other retailers where all together in one power center with the usual shadow tenants that follow the anchors into a location. Our city was known locally and regionally for being a bedroom community to Tulsa and nearly a third of our residents had moved here to be near the airport where American Airlines had a maintenance base that was the employment center for these folks and lots of others in this area. Our city population inside the city limits was just over 13,000 people. Our "fence line" or school district population was a few thousand more, but for the most part we were considered a small town.

However, after I began to look at where our consumers were coming from, and the amount of sales that were generated by our small group of retailers, some interesting data began to surface. The first thing that stuck out was the amount of retail sales in comparison with the population of our community was shocking in itself. It was plainly obvious that our population in itself could not produce the volume of retail sales that we were seeing. When we looked at zip code data what we found was that our city was pulling consumers in from over 20 other cities located around us. What became clear was that due to a unique alignment of several state and national highways, consumer traffic in route to our urban core of Tulsa was "funneled" right through the middle of our community.

I grew up in northeast Texas and had seen first-hand what had transpired in communities like McKinney and Rockwall, Texas. McKinney sits to the north of urban Dallas and Rockwall geographically is due east of the Dallas metro area. These two communities were small, insignificant farming towns that literally got covered in national retail over a relatively short period of time, due to some substantial residential growth, but more so because of their geography as a doorway or "portal" city where out of area consumers accessed the big retail and restaurant brands in metro Dallas. I realized at that point that Owasso was the beneficiary of the exact same phenomenon and that if we could provide data that proved this theory that we might very well have a chance to procure a great deal of private sector investment and create some sizable sales tax growth for our city's general fund revenue. Also the City of Owasso was fortunate to have some considerable flood plain on our south fence-line with Tulsa that would prevent the City of Tulsa from incentivizing major retail development between the two markets. Over the last several decades Tulsa had strategically created retail districts on the portal or border of their city limits with Broken Arrow, Jenks, Bixby, Glenpool, Sapulpa, and Sand Springs; all of which are first ring suburbs of Tulsa. These shopping districts intentionally and purposefully drew sales tax dollars away from these suburbs into Tulsa's jurisdiction as residents and consumers from these suburbs shopped at Tulsa retail and restaurant locations. Owasso also benefitted from industrial and manufacturing and non-retail zoning in Tulsa County that caused even more of a shield for our community against retail development from Tulsa to our south. People responsible for economic development in any community should at least attempt to locate retail development in areas that would allow for the most exposure to consumers coming into or through their local market from outside the city limits. The wise use of incentives sometimes allows for development of sales tax producing retail development in these areas that pull outside consumers or regional trade into the local market. In small or

61

rural markets, other things such as recreational and historic locations, as well as local festivals or gatherings, properly advertised can do a great deal to pull retail trade into a local market.

When I started to compile this data, I began to see that our small city had actually a lot more potential than we had realized before. We actually had a market potential of over 10-15 times what our population was, and the premium sales that our very few retailers were producing annually was a direct validation of that fact. In *"City on a Hill"*,

> **Learning to evaluate time, and discern the nuances of time is critical to success.**

I outlined the sequence of events that actually happened in Owasso, and people who have read the book and especially those who have worked in development of retail product have mentioned to me that the ingredients to the retail explosion that happened here all peaked at the right time. Timing is crucial to a lot of things. I get a little peeved from time to time talking to city administrators and elected officials who just don't seem to have a sense of urgency when they talk about the future of their community. Time does a lot of strange things. They say time heals everything. That's not necessarily true. They say time keeps marching on. That is true. Learning to evaluate time, and discern the nuances of time is critical to success. In retail development sometimes time kills deals. Let me give you some real world examples. If you plant a tree you must realize that there is a 50-50 chance that the tree will survive the process of natural growth with the sun, and rain, and day and night, and winter, spring, summer, and fall. You understand there are seasons, and as seasons change, the process of living and growing continues for the tree. So let's say that the tree survives and one pretty springtime day, you notice buds on the tree. The buds cause quite a stir, and folks begin to notice and an anticipation for fruit begins to build in the community. Time passes and soon there is fruit hanging on every branch of the tree. Keep in mind all the time maintenance is required, and those who are the harvesters better discern the times, because if you pick the fruit too early, it's not good. And just as important, if you pick the fruit too late it over ripens and is no good. It doesn't matter that you didn't understand and appreciate time...nevertheless timing is everything to get the fruit to market. There is a process to development. There are seasons in growth for just about everything on the planet. The sooner you become aware of the process, and respect the process, and learn to cooperate with the process and keep all the plates spinning the sooner you can see fruit.

Another way to look at this issue of timing is to compare the scenario the next time you book a flight on a commercial airline. They will tell you when your flight is supposed to depart. Those of you that have flown a lot know already that very rarely does a flight leave the exact time the airline promised. Now I know they do the best they can, but I have sat patiently through long delays, even sometimes missing a connecting flight. I can't lie to you...I have never been patient about anything. But you get the picture. In addition to delays, try to slow play a commercial airline and see if they will wait on you. Let me just tell you up front, and I know this by personal experience. They will leave you if you don't conform to their timetable. So when retail development is forming or staging in your community, your community must react with some sense of timing. If you try to force a deal to speed up, it will probably stall. If you pull an incentive because you don't like the retailer or the developer's timing, the deal will probably stall or cave in. On the other hand, if the city's own development process is so bureaucratic that it causes major time delays in a project, the project can stall or fail to come to fruition. My experience shows that this happens much more than cities want to admit. Just recently in Tulsa, a national recreational retailer revealed their interest in the Tulsa market, first store for this particular retailer in Oklahoma. When the site was revealed, a storm of protest erupted and eventually a lawsuit was filed, and well over a year later the issues have still not been resolved. There is no way to recover from just the lost sales tax that this retailer would have generated if the development plan would have been seamless and time sensitive.

Timing is everything. To the private sector timing delays and slowdowns can costs hundreds of thousands of dollars. In a very real way cities suffer also, especially when the economics of a regional retailer, which would pull out of market consumers into town and generate much sales and ad valorem taxes for the city is delayed.

There are some communities that have more potential than others. But all towns and cities, whether they are rural, suburban, or densely populated urban centers have potential to grow, and grow the right way; if they can comprehend and understand the process. I can tell you without hesitation that Owasso, Oklahoma had potential to grow when I came here. All the ingredients were in the mix, all the stars were lined up, and for a moment in time, we had a chance to lasso the potential and put it all where it needed to go. Let me say at this juncture that as I have traveled all over the country and spoke with city after city, I have been asked many times if what happened here literally happened "overnight". No development of any size happens "overnight". It took over two decades to get the city in a place where it could grow, and even after all the stars where lined up, it still took over eight years to see the retail growth come. I still look at city councilors who get behind a microphone at a public meeting, and say "you've been working for us for a year or so and we haven't seen anything" as a special kind of ignorant. Economic development in any genre takes TIME. Lots of time.

In my work in Owasso, after we had determined that nearly 65% of our sales tax

---

Economic development in any genre takes TIME. Lots of time.

---

revenues were coming from outside of market consumers we set out to begin to prepare market data and materials that would provide that narrative to developers and retail and restaurant brands at the national level. Once a city gains the knowledge that their trade area populace is perhaps much larger than their population in the city limits and the evidence is there to actually verify the market strength with real world data, then the fun starts. I run into city people, whether they are on the administrative side or an elected official, who have spent large amounts of public money with data companies that provide really slick reports, lots of graphs, statistics, "psychographic" mumbo jumbo, and other non-realistic drivel. Our company has been hired many times after one of these data generators (my competitors) has left the city high and dry after a three year engagement. Data without a back story that collaborates the energy of the market, the potential of the market, and the depth of the retail market is just numbers. And what my competitors don't always want to discuss is the fact that no matter how rich or how lean the market may be, in any retail deal there is a real estate transaction of some kind involved. And if you understand anything about a real estate transaction, you know that at any point along the way the deal can blow completely up. After having been involved in hundreds of retail specific transactions, these deals can fall apart for a good reason, a bad reason, or for no reason at all. Again to stay on the theme of this chapter, there are many reasons why retail development takes so long. Cities should take into consideration that once this practice of pushing your market data out on a national scale begins, that the process is just beginning.

In our community, retail development absolutely changed the city's future. Retail development changed the entire course of where our city had been, where it was, and ultimately changed the future of our community in a drastic way. The process and the story of what happened in Owasso is the subject of my book, "*City On A Hill*". When I wrote the book, I told the story in general terms but did not get into very much detail on the ebb and flow, the back and forth, the thrill of victory and the deep agony of all the setbacks in that process. Instead of doing my job as an experienced economic development guy I became a consummate expert in putting out fires and solving problems every few minutes for several years. When your community gets going in the development process, all kinds of issues come out and they have to be dealt with. These issues, many of them seemingly minor, can and did bring a halt to deals every few days. I learned to anticipate problems before they happened. It is necessary to be proactive. Believe me. Even with me and our team totally fixated on keeping the private sector investment running efficiently, it still took over eight years to finish our retail core. Keep in mind that in 2002-2007 retailers and restaurants were aggressively growing. Walmart was doing a couple hundred new units a year, Target was doing 100-150 units a year, Home Depot and Lowe's were doing a hundred units. With these big box anchors doing this much growing, the junior anchors and pad users, small shop tenants, and those that fill in the gaps were following them just as aggressively. The national economy was strong, banks were literally throwing money at retail deals, and cities were putting big incentive packages together and developing public/private partnerships that insured these deals went as smoothly and quickly as possible. All the stars where lined up perfectly. There was an absolutely perfect environment for massive growth. But my point in saying all this is that even in that perfect environment, it still took eight years. How long will development take then in less than perfect environments? LONGER.

In our situation in Owasso, the first phase of development took over two years because that is how long it took to get Target to see our community as a viable site. When Target pulled the trigger, it only took a few more months to get another half million feet of national tenants to agree to come. After the initial power center that was anchored by Target, Belk, and Hobby Lobby developed, we were out of real estate. Big boy tenants were wanting to come to Owasso, but we were out of land in this phase. Tenants like Best

Buy literally where told, they should have pulled the trigger earlier, because now they are going to have to wait. We had to get more land, move more utilities and public infrastructure, and relocate service industries like a natural gas maintenance facility that was sitting on some of the most pristine retail real estate you could imagine. It took several months to do each part of what I just described.

This process is slow. Are you starting to see a pattern? You cannot have a situation where all the obvious and non-obvious potential problems are dealt with. You just have to keep grinding. So you can now see why it is necessary to educate city folks and elected officials. The private sector knows full well how long this process takes. The public sector is a different story. Government in any form moves very slowly. That is why I always applaud communities that are at least attempting to be proactive.

I also am pleased to be able to say that **every** community that the Retail Attractions team has worked with, and that has stayed the course, and endured the process I have just described to you has been the recipient of new retail and the corresponding new sales tax, and ad valorem taxes that new retail development brings with it when it comes. But believe me, it is a very frustrating thing to have to listen to people whine about how long the process takes.

Recently The National Real Estate Investor magazine posted an article online that I saw on social media that told a story of a regional mall project that had been in some stage of development for over eighteen (18) years. The deal had passed from developer to developer, and had over a billion dollars thrown at it over the years with no opening date in sight. Not long ago a New Jersey local finance board gave the green light to use $800 million in high risk bonds to help the current developer finish the project by mid-2018. It is freaky to even imagine that a retail deal could take that long.

Let me take a moment and just list a few of the things that have to happen to see a new retail or restaurant deal happen in your town. First there has to be proof in some manner that your market will generate premium sales for the retailer. In small markets that process alone may take months. When the retailer shows interest in a particular location the site analysis and site comparisons begin, traffic flow is studied, traffic counts are obtained, and the site is analyzed for its development readiness. There is soil testing, environmental screening, storm water and hydrological studies are done. The availability of public utilities are evaluated and attention to detail is critical because I have seen retail sites rejected because there was not enough water pressure to adequately supply fire protection and sprinklers. There are engineering and architectural plans done. There are meetings after meetings to discuss landscaping requirements, allowed signage, lot setback requirements, actual construction materials and construction methods used are evaluated. Bids are requested and prices negotiated. The real estate transaction itself may take months to close. Any real estate or title issues have to be cured. Financing has to be procured. There is platting, zoning, and annexation issues to contend with. Developers many times have to face hostile home owners and mean city planners. Sometimes building pads or lots have to go through a lot-split procedure or sometimes easements, right of way issues, covenants, and restrictions have to be dealt with. Moving or relocating public utility infrastructure takes forever and sometimes adds tons of costs to the deal. Developers have to negotiate tenant improvements, lease language and terms, and deal with subcontractors. And I am only scratching the surface. Most of the time Murphy's Law comes in to play. According to Wikipedia "Murphy's Law" is a popular adage that states that "things will go wrong in any given situation, if you give them a chance," or more commonly, "whatever can go wrong, will go wrong." This is a law that works as sure as the law of gravity, especially in economic development.

Bottom line, this process takes a long time. If you are a student of development you will soon learn that all deals are fragile. They have to be hand carried and protected. Retail development is cyclic. It cycles around and saturates markets then declination infects the market and then the cycle starts all over. I learned this lesson the hard way. I started my consulting company after the retail boom in Owasso had opened doors for me to meet literally hundreds of retail and development professionals. I started listening to them, and learning from them with many of the people I met telling me that there was a niche here between the public and private sectors. So when the retail explosion happened here I decided to leave my cushy job at the city, (with great insurance benefits, a stellar retirement, take home car, flexible hours and great pay) and start Retail Attractions, LLC, an economic and retail development consulting firm in October of 2007. If you have any memory at all, up until the fall of 2007 it was a seemingly perfect time to step out and start my new company. But then in the spring of 2008 what happened? The biggest economic recession since the "Great Depression" occurred. And for about three years retail development all but stopped. I went through depression, despair, and fear for several weeks, until a friend of mine spoke these encouraging words to me. He said, "Rickey, welcome to the private sector. You don't work for the government anymore. Out here you can feast and starve in the same year. Go ahead and grab the tiger by the tail. And when you come out of this, you will have a story to tell your grandchildren. You can tell them I grabbed the tiger by the tail, and won. Or you can tell them how you lost your arm. Either way it will be a great story."

Development of anything from its origin to grand opening will take longer than anybody involved thinks it will.

SO I am still here. With both arms. What has happened to me still amazes me. I have been able to travel and work literally all over the country, from Manhattan to Los Angeles, from Mandan, North Dakota to McAllen, Texas. I have met hundreds of city managers, city councilors, aldermen, trustees, economic development professionals. I've worked with hundreds of retail people from corporate real estate people, to tenant representatives from big and small brokerage firms. I have worked with some of the best developers of retail real estate, shopping centers, and outlet malls in the world.

And the one thing I can swear to after all these years is this....this business takes a long time. Development of anything from its origin to its grand opening will take longer than anybody involved thinks it will. That is a fact.

If you're reading this and you work for a public sector entity in any capacity in economic development; relax and let the process produce the product. First the sowing then the reaping.

Let me give you a sequential look at a typical series of events that occurs in commercial real estate development. The following list is made up of the general items that take place, but don't let the simplicity of it lull you into believing that the process is simple. It is anything but simple. It can go haywire at any of these sequential steps. From start to finish can take months for the fortunate ones, and many years for the less fortunate.

Typical development process for commercial real estate:

1. Identify real estate or asset.
2. Purchase land or asset.
3. Assess general economic climate & conditions.
4. Access and obtain financing.
5. Assess the space markets & determine how much space is needed.
6. Understand demographics & social & political forces.
7. Develop a master plan for site.
8. Design buildings and interiors.
9. Obtain entitlements and permits.
10. Construct the project.
11. Lease the project.
12. Operate and maintain project.
13. Decide whether to sell or hold asset.

Let me say again so there is absolutely no confusion. This process sounds very simplistic and almost fool proof. Make no mistake about it, this process is filled with risks and lots of drama. Variables such as retail growth strategies, real estate trends, greed, building material pricing and availability, availability and prices of sub-contractors and specialty trades, NIMBYs and CAVE people, availability of real estate, landowner's pricing of real estate and whether or not to sell, zoning and annexation issues, storm water issues on site, weather, visibility and access issues, city codes and regulatory bureaucratic immovability, and literally a ton of other unnamed trouble and woe that can drop down on a deal from a clear blue sky.

But when all the stars align and your city is the beneficiary of a solid retail deal with great tenants, there is revenue, and more than that there is an immediate quality of life boost to the community.

Final word.... Our company can help your city. And let me say this although it sounds like I'm bragging. EVERY community that has hired us, and stayed with us through this process has new retail. Every one. Some cities saw it in the first year. Others it took three or four years. But the ones who stuck it out, all of them benefitted and we left them in a better place than we found them. Let us help your community change its future for the better.

CHAPTER 3

PUBLIC SECTOR HORROR STORIES

Just in case you think all the horror stories are in the movies, I wanted to just share a few honest to goodness stories that didn't make the big screen. They certainly would have made the press if they had been successful and maybe they should have been reported so people could see just how twisted the public sector can get. I will leave further comments to the smart guys. One thing I know these events occurred and I witnessed them first hand. I will not identify the participants or the cities in which these events happened. But the fact that they happened prove that cities and those who work for them: city managers, mayors and city councilors, and city staff sometimes do really stupid things.

The first incident that I will share involved the first phase of a shopping center in Oklahoma that involved a site where a Target anchored power center was being developed. The first phase included Target (obviously), Hobby Lobby, and Belk with another 400,000 square feet of junior anchors like Pier One, TJ Maxx, Linens and Things, Lane Bryant, Old Navy, Rue

21, Claire's, Dress Barn, Men's Wearhouse, Kirkland's, a couple of hotels, and a few national restaurants. Toward the end of the construction phase, I was meeting regularly with the general contractor and the developer to discuss construction issues and problems. My job was chief problem solver and issue corrector. It was in one of these meetings that I was reviewing a report and budget reconciliation on actual construction costs. Since there were public incentives involved in the project, I had to monitor the construction costs to see if the bids, and the final costs aligned. In the process of reviewing the reports I came across a line item simply titled "unnecessary project costs-Marcus". [Marcus is a fake name to protect the public sector employee]. I asked the general contractor what that item was for. The budget was over $50,000 for this line item. The contractor went to the file cabinet in the construction trailer and put a manila folder on the table. As I looked through the folder, I saw invoice after invoice, and change order after change order where this public sector employee had ordered the contractor to tear out perfectly good items that were just a few inches off the planned location. The resulting tearing out required new construction to satisfy this inspector. When I began to press about the demolition and redo of these items, what the contractor told me embarrassed me initially, then made me angry. I asked for an explanation of why this was not shared with me when it happened. The GC said he thought it was just something that had to be done. I questioned him about whether what the inspector did effected the overall development in a negative way, and his response was that the original construction of the public infrastructure in question was moved a few inches from where the plans called for to save some of the costs. Without going into a great deal of explanation what was happening in a nutshell was a city inspector just being mean and unnecessarily bureaucratic. I made copies of the invoices and work orders and showed them to the city manager. He was aghast about the situation as I was and ultimately the inspector was replaced and was given his pink slip. This is an example of proper authority being used in a very improper way. Common sense and being business friendly would have saved time and money for all involved. When a public sector employee goes nuts on the letter of the law, instead of using a little discretion and common sense, it costs the private sector money and time.

While I am not saying that cities should just let the private sector go about their development with no oversight, I am saying that partnering with the private sector to save costs, alleviate risk, and shouldering the responsibility to protect public funds is a win – win scenario for both sides of the deal.

The next occurrence happened in a mid-sized market in Texas that had a ton of momentum going for them when they hired our company. Midway into our first year of a two-year contract with the city, a large mixed use deal began to take shape. There was a planned hybrid amusement park / water park / retail and hospitality site being planned on a large site owned by the city. The development would have drawn consumers into the market from an extremely large radius and would have meant millions upon millions of dollars of property, sales, and hotel / motel taxes to the city. The deal was taking shape, and when it became time for the city officials to begin to meet to discuss incentives and other strategy on the site, out of the clear blue sky the city attorney called the city manager and me into a meeting and simply said this deal is dead. It seems that when the city attorney began his due diligence on the project, looking through reams of paper planning and laying out the business side of the deal he discovered that one of the ownership LLC's involved in the deal was a partnership between the mayor and his sons. He was shocked as were the manager and I that a deal that would have been great for the city was tanked because of a conflict of interest. Needless to say the mayor is not with the city anymore, and the site is still empty.

This next event was so bizarre that it took me and the development group involved a few weeks just to process what happened. In a large suburban market in Oklahoma a new Walmart Super Center was planned for a site that held some potential to bring other retail and hospitality uses and other mixed uses to the city. In the planning stages and meetings with the city manager and staff to discuss a public / private partnership between the city and the developer, the city, in the course of the discussions promised to fund a road widening project that the anchor retailer had insisted on prior to agreeing to come to the site. All the discussions were going well and the relationship between the city's development staff and the developer was growing. It looked like a successful development that would have generated tons of sales tax revenue to the city's general fund was well underway and going as planned. Toward the time site work was finishing and the foundation and construction of the new anchor retailer were beginning, the city announced a new bond package that would see several miles of new roads constructed and new public infrastructure and had even set a date for the bond package vote. After the bond was approved by a vote of the citizens, construction had begun on the anchor and I was asked by the developer to check with the city and see if any other issues needed to be addressed. A quick meeting with city manager and community development staff for the city indicated no issues. After a week or two, there was an article in the local newspaper about the bond package funding and how the funds from the bond package were going to be distributed. I scoured the newspaper article for the road package the city had agreed to in a public meeting and had promised to fund to keep the public side of the agreement to satisfy the anchor tenant request for a new access road for the retail center. Not seeing the project in question mentioned, I wasn't immediately alarmed because sometimes the public sector "hides" projects in a larger omnibus type of funding package. So I called the community development office at the city and spoke to the director of that office, simply in an effort to see which pot of funding the city was going to use to do the road project for the retail center that was promised and publicly approved by the city council. He acted confused and said he would check with the city attorney and the manager's office to see where the appropriate funding would come from and get back to me. I waited for another two weeks, received no call or information from the city, so I called back. This time the development services director told me that the city had decided not to do the road project at all, and had used the funds they had promised to the retail center to do other projects the manager's office had deemed more important. I reminded the public sector employee that the developer had a signed development agreement and city council had approved the funding for the retail project in a public meeting. The employee stated that the decision not to do the road project was made "above his pay grade" and that there was nothing he could do about it. I advised him that if he stepped outside in a few minutes that he would be able to hear a developer calling the curses of God down on his city from a hundred miles away. In looking at this now, the city promised to do something, publicly approved the package in a public meeting and then completely reneged on the deal leaving the anchor tenant and the developer hanging. The tenant's decision to do the deal on the site in question was contingent on the road widening. The city promised to do it, the developer did what he promised, the retailer did what they promised, and then the city decided simply that we are not going to honor their end of the commitment. To this date, the anchor tenant is open on the site, but other shadow development has not occurred as planned because of the inadequate access to the site. Too bad for the city. This is another reason why people don't trust the government. Needless to say the city manager is not there anymore, and life goes on. But one thing is for sure, you can bet that the developer has shared with colleagues in his profession that the city in question is anathema for developers. Count on that.

Another event occurred in a town where our company had worked for three years. Retail Attractions had been fortunate enough to facilitate over half a dozen new retail deals there, and a much larger deal was in the works anchored by a sporting goods retailer and including some junior anchor tenants that the city needed to grow its retail base. The executive director of the local Economic Development Corporation was a great friend of mine who had done a tremendous job of laying foundational groundwork that would over the course of the next few years put this city on the map with manufacturers, industrial plants, and with the retailers and restaurants who would have come to this growing and very underserved market. He had built consensus among the local land owners, and stakeholders and was literally putting this old community back in the limelight again. In the midst of this growth potential an election was held and somehow a local physician was elected to an open city council seat. Keep in mind he got elected by about thirty votes when only about 50 votes were even cast in the entire election. When he got elected this goofball, worked behind the scenes to get elected mayor by his peers on the council, mainly because no one else wanted to be mayor. Being mayor had no special authority, just the ability to sign official documents and welcome folks to the community. In a short time he had successfully changed city staff meetings to his own private office outside of city hall, had a parking place painted on the street in front of city hall with a sign saying that no one could park there except for himself. He made it a habit to come a couple of minutes late to council meetings so he could rush up to his private parking place and rush into the meetings with great fan fair to the delight of his minions. This individual recruited some confederates and pretty soon he brought a false and misleading attack on the economic development director that resulted in a hostile takeover of the economic development corporation's board of directors. And in just a few weeks a gentlemen who had worked tirelessly to make needed changes to a tired old city's economic development efforts and who was finally making much progress was out on his ear. The issues were all blown out of proportion, many outright lies were discovered later, and litigation was threatened but to no avail. The vision planted by the economic developer was destroyed and the city went back to its old "good old boys in the back room making the decisions" days. Luckily a vote to take all the money away from the EDC, instigated by this goofy mayor, was overturned by a vote of the locals. But the town is still a mess, and still not headed in the right direction. Public sector people need to recognize when an elected official is acting outside the scope of the office and call them down or replace them.

The next incident happened to me in a town I worked in a few years ago when one of the city councilors was facing not being re-elected and decided that before he was removed from office that he would use his considerable influence to fire all the consultants. The next thing I knew my contract was not renewed and in a couple of weeks it was announced in the media that the councilor had resigned and became a consultant to the city doing economic development. Now I know you are just going to think I am a disgruntled consultant, upset because an unqualified individual got my goat and took my place. That's really not what upset me about this deal at all. The fact is I had worked hard for this little town, gotten them some new retail, and really I never take a contract renewal or the lack of getting renewed personally. I promise you my source of income is not limited to the decisions of people on city councils. My source of income is the same as everybody else's. The good Lord takes care of me and my family. There has not been one time when we had to beg for bread. If I was dependent on men for my sustenance I would be worried sick. What really ticked me off was that the first retail deal that came to this town after I left [by the way I had been working with this specific retailer for over two years about the market in this story], went to a site owned by the new guy's family. When the public sector employees are major land owners in the community, it gets a little dicey sometimes. This doesn't pass muster with the watchdogs who keep tabs on development and really is a dangerous precedent for the city, and could open them up to litigation.

Another suburban market hired our firm a few years back after working with some of our so called competitors who did not perform after three years, and we were quickly able to get the attention of a couple of national level developers and interest them in a couple of local sites. One developer put a site under contract, and began working with tenants and it soon became apparent that there was major interest in the market from a few retailers. As the deal talks progressed the city began to ask questions about public private partnerships, and rightly so because this deal was going to require a significant contribution of public funds. One day it dawned on me that to get a public / private partnership done it would require a super-majority vote by the city council. This means that the vote had to pass by 4-1 vote and could not simply pass by a 3-2 vote. As we looked further it was revealed that the site in question was actually owned by the mayor, and believe it or not his broker in the deal was his vice-mayor on the city council. I alerted the city and the developer to this situation. It came as no surprise to me that when my contract came up for renewal the city manager asked me to work for the city for another year, but because of his situation he couldn't pay me, but lucky for me he said he would "make me whole" on the backside of the retail deal. I reminded him because of his situation with the current city council a deal was not going to happen. Then I offered him a deal instead, I told him I would work for him and his city free, if he would also work the next twelve months for free. I reminded him that his city had just finished a three-year contract with a group that was paid a large sum of money and that the city had received no benefit at all. He said he couldn't do that and I simply replied, "me neither". I said I agreed to work for you at a reduced rate because I was fairly close to the community, and in the first year I had multiple developers attempting to purchase real estate for developing real retail deals. I don't think he ever put the "two + two" together. The land is still vacant.

I have a multitude of other stories I could tell you about some of the other cities we have worked in. Let me just say that strange things happen both in the public and the private sector. In the public sector however there are some sensitivities that simply will not pass public muster. City folks, city managers, mayors, elected officials, city staff, all public sector folks are under a tremendous amount of scrutiny and they will be in the future as well. But when it comes to the very appearance of someone on the public sector side doing something, whether it is completely innocent or as sinister as all get out, it is going to be looked at with great scrutiny by the many watchdog groups active in today's events, especially those on social media. It doesn't matter if they are liberals from the farther reaches of the left or fanatical right wing zealots who hate everybody from the other side. They are watching the public sector with tremendous intensity. My advice to anyone thinking about running for any public office is to make sure your closet containing all the nasties of your past is locked good and tight. You can also be mayor and own all the land you want, but it is not kosher to own the land in a retail deal that is going to have public money in it while you are mayor. It may in fact be legal as buying a coke, but it looks incredibly bad to the people watching from the sidelines. Using local politics for one's apparent personal advantage is not ever going to be accepted without some controversy. Whether it's legal or not.

Let's end this chapter on a happy note. One of the things we attempt to do in all the cities we work in is to have the public sector reach out to the faith community in the city. Getting all the pastors and church leaders behind your work is important for a number of reasons. One, it gives the public sector a great vehicle for sharing community information. If the faith community is doing its job, they will relish the opportunity to yoke together with the city to support the agenda of improving the quality of life. And last but not least, we all need all the prayers we can get. I know I do.

Not everything the government does is bad, they do lots of good things as well. What it's all about is transparency, accessibility, and financial responsibility. IF the public sector is focused and working hard to insure that these three things are the foundation of all they do, everything will flow where it needs to flow.

When the public sector is working with the private sector it is always good to listen respectfully, then let your yays be yays and your nays be nays. In other words, do what you say you will do. Public / private partnerships are going to be more and more important as time goes on.

Nasty politics are always going to be a part of the development landscape. They (politicians and their political maneuvering) will be an obstacle that is not going to go away. And it will always take more time than you can imagine to do economic development, no matter what level it's done on. Details of retail deals must be kept confidential until the specifics of the deal are worked out, contracts and tenant leases are signed, and the finished product is open for business. The language of retail development needs to be a part of the public sector's vocabulary so we can see these deals from the private sector's side and understand the inherent risk, and pressure developers are under to get retail and restaurant deals open, and what the dark side is if and when these deals fold and fail to make.

Thank you for your attention, and for your purchase of this book. I love my job and wouldn't trade it for the world. I love driving through a city and seeing retail deals that our company has worked on in the community. I kind of feel like our company has marked the city, made it a little bit better in terms of the quality of life benefits and revenue that the finished product brings to the city.

Last but not least. If you desire new retail in your community, if you need to increase your revenue stream, if certain types of retail goods and services are not available in your town, hire a professional. Hiring Retail Attractions, LLC will save you time and money in the long run.

CHAPTER 4

"WE ARE NOT LIKE THEM"

If you're still reading you are probably either really curious or desperate. If you have had the pleasure of working around cities as long as I have you already know some curious stuff goes on when politics and money, lust and greed, and the carnal side of humans is involved in any endeavor. And if you have worked on the public sector side of development, or in the public sector in any way, you have probably been desperate a time or two.

Everyone knows the private sector and the public sector are very different. They have different goals and different objectives and different motives. They are governed by completely different principles. The actionable oversight of the public sector is absolutely unique from the private sector. Obviously the private sector has more freedom to operate, while public sector organizations are governed by codes, regulations, different laws, rules, "traditions" and sometimes nasty politics. I have actually been scolded by a city attorney who said in a public meeting, "I don't give a damn how other cities do this, we do things our own way here."

The differences are distinct but let me sum up few of them for you here as simply as I can:

1. **The goals of the public sector are different from the goals of the private sector.** The public sector is focused on serving the immediate and long-range needs of the community, the development of revenue streams to fund basic public needs and services, and creating and improving the nebulous "quality of life" factor. The private sector's immediate and fundamental concern is a quality return on investment. Profit drives the private sector. Also the private sector must answer to their investors, stakeholders, and customers. Public sector entities may be able to survive inefficient operation, while poorly ran private sector organizations can go broke and have to close the doors. While the public sector is or should be focused on public scrutiny, social media and special interest groups are always available to point a finger at "miss-management" and political promises are fast becoming as meaningless as the other stuff on

television and radio. You have to be tough to work in the public sector. At the end of the day, the difference in goals and the way both sectors are affected by external forces are poles apart. I live in Oklahoma and I love the people here, but if the State of Oklahoma was a business, we would be broke and unemployed. Whose fault is that? It's the politicians fault. ☺ In the private sector if you screw something up, you get replaced.

2. **The way the public sector hires employees is different from the private sector.** In the public sector a longer hiring process is involved because to create a position and fund the position may take several months. Also to fill an empty position takes longer on the government side. In the private sector, companies have the ability to hire quickly depending on the business cycle and the need for more personnel. On the flip side private sector administrators can fire and offer severance packages to employees at any time. Public sector human resources encounter a good deal of bureaucratic red tape, requiring

extensive documentation and making the removal process more complex and time consuming.

3. **The procurement process is more drawn out in the public sector.** Since public entities are funded by tax revenue, which is generated by the public or through the issuance of public debt, the whole process of procurement is not directly controlled internally. Public funding must be obtained and disbursed, and the procurement process must get approved by multiple levels of oversight, all of which slows down the procurement process considerably. Companies in the private sector benefit from a much quicker procurement process. Private organizations are able to use their revenue from sales and investments to purchase real estate, and other goods and services when they need them. They are also less encumbered by regulations dictating supplier relationships, allowing them to get better deals and renew existing contracts to speed up the process. Most, if not all public sector purchases require competitive bidding, requests for

qualifications and requests for proposals for services which all add time to the process.

4. **Public organizations face unique accountability.** Governmental entities are subject to a specific kind of scrutiny. This is mainly due to the fact that they are funded by taxpayers who hold these public agencies accountable for how their money is being spent and who view each expenditure not only for their efficiency and effectiveness but also for the degree that these purchases address questions of social equality and fairness. The activities and accomplishments of these public entities hold a greater interest in the court of public opinion. Leaders of private companies and corporations are not accustomed to this level of scrutiny because they are primarily responsible to investors, boards of directors, and shareholders.

5. **Public organizations often can't choose their goals.** In the private sector, businesses set their own goals and focus their resources on accomplishing them. The goals are set with the aim of

achieving profits and capturing market share and are the result of company strategy. Public organizations continuously find themselves pressed by legislative mandates, facing outside forces, and often have to try to accommodate a host of other organizations or special interest groups that can have conflicting goals. Public officials and political parties establish agendas on specific issues that advance their interests and keep them winning elections and in office. In this way, the goals of a public organization can see big changes driven by electoral politics.

Public and private organizations face challenges that are unique to each sector. Leadership in both spheres requires specific abilities for achieving their goals.

Public & private organizations face challenges that are unique to each sector.

While private sector managers often benefit from analytical thinking, business savvy and creative marketing techniques, public administrators who wish to excel require a deep understanding of laws governing municipal government, and strong communication and interpersonal skills in addition to the business-oriented skills of a private sector manager.

Elected officials are not required to have any specific skill sets or training and many times set policy based on emotions or other factors that will not carry the weight and pressure of growth, regulatory oversight, and public opinion. These differences were the primary motivation to me to start our company in an effort to be a liaison between the two groups and help both get to the revenue and get a return on investment for both sectors.

You may be asking at this point what difference all this makes. Let me just say that in the current makeover of the retail industry the private sector takes a whole different view of risk. When I was being educated on the retail industry, the times were completely different than today. Almost every retailer was in growth mode. Some were taking inordinate risks, and for some brands the result was tremendous profits. For others the result was overbuilding, the credit issues that came from the overbuilding, and bankruptcy and closing of stores. Either way retailers were growing and there was a great chance that if you were working in a community that was growing in population, your community was seeing retail deals happen on a regular basis. Capital was easy to obtain, and retailers and restaurants and developers were busy doing deals. "Big box" development enabled large tracts of real estate to be developed and Walmart and Target anchored power centers were popping up all over the country. For smaller communities, a new Walmart Supercenter was the answer to their present and future revenue needs.

Well time changes everything. Currently Walmart is not doing much, if any. No new Targets, Home Depots, and Lowe's. Retail is done completely different today and each of the few deals that are getting done are done with much more oversight and scrutiny. And let me tell you what else is involved in 99% of new retail deals. Some sort of public / private partnership. The benefits of this type of partnership are obvious. Both the public and private sectors enjoy quicker turnarounds on projects, risk abatement, costs savings, and other mutual benefits. I've preached since I started working in this arena that cities should treat the private sector like customers instead of being bureaucratic and so hard to get along with. The synergy created by partnering allows both sides to obtain a better finished product than either could produce on their own.

One of the most frustrating and difficult parts of my work is to stand in front of a panel of elected officials and city administrators and staff and explain the process of retail development or economic development for that matter. Society as a whole has been brainwashed and seduced by what I call the "myth of instant gratification". No matter how intelligent and educated people are, for the most part we are taught to believe that we are special and that we deserve special treatment and that the rules everybody else has to play by do not apply to us. When cities deal with the private sector, they realize really quickly that a capricious and arbitrary attitude simply will not get you very far. Or at least they should realize that. I have sat at meetings with both public and private sectors, in urban communities with hefty populations, where the public sector reps try to impress a developer or a large retailer that their community is absolutely the best place in the world for the developer or retailer to build a shopping center or open a new unit. In one particular meeting in a large city in Oklahoma (you can probably guess because there are only two) the developer was sharing with the public sector how hard it was to get big boy retailers to come to tertiary markets and how difficult it was to get deals financed. The public sector folks thought the developer was talking about some of the micropolitan and suburban markets around the state. They were aghast when he shared with him that their market was the one he was referring to. There are no boomtowns in Oklahoma. In fact there are only about nine real growth nodes in the country and the closest to Oklahoma is the Dallas / Fort Worth metroplex. I shared this story in *"City On A Hill"* about an experience at the ICSC conference in Las Vegas in 2013. I was contracted to a suburb of one of Oklahoma's large markets, and the city manager of that community told me that if I could get him a meeting with Lowe's, that he could convince them in 15 minutes that his suburban market was the absolute best place in the country for a new Lowe's. So I got a meeting with a broker and a Lowe's corporate real estate guy, that had done the majority of all the Lowe's deals in our state and for fifteen minutes the city manager made his case. At the end of his tirade, the real estate guy thanked me for setting up the meeting. As we were standing up from the table, the real estate guy looks at the city manager and tells him, "Sir, I appreciate your candidness, but the fact is I have five hundred cities on our radar that are better markets for us than your community."

Almost all modern retail deals require some form of public incentive to make the deal work.

Telling elected officials and city staff that incentives are required get me in trouble all the time. I get every excuse in the book from "WE don't do incentives." to "Why should we give public money to these greedy developers?", to "We did not have to incentivize these retailers that are already here, why are they required on this deal?". The truth is that in almost all modern retail deals some form of public incentive is going to be required to make the deal work. And I will promise you that if your city is unwilling, the city down the road will do them, and the retail deal and all the sales tax and ad valorem revenues that the deal generates will go to the city with the incentives.

When cities see how long the process takes in real time, it becomes apparent that getting retail done requires a really huge investment of time, patience, and hard work by lots of people. When I am asked about what happened to Owasso, Oklahoma, most of the time people simply assume that the deals just fell together and we were overnight successes. It took eight years in some of the best economic times in history, and nobody really realizes until I educate them that three decades before the retail came the City of Owasso was preparing, running sanitary sewer and water lines, buying right of way, engineering and planning for growth, and setting policy that would make Owasso a real "business-friendly" community when the time was right.

Another thing that public sector people should certainly understand is that when a developer or retail or restaurant comes looking is that they have their own data. Never believe that the city propaganda that city after city shares with potential developers or tenants is what convinces them to come. In fact, let me say it in the plainest way possible. The private sector knows your market data inside and out and be assured that they will always know your town better than you do. I am not saying that local knowledge is not important, it certainly is. But do not ever believe that your pretty pictures and marketing materials are the key to retailers finding a site in your town. Retail development is a very relationship based business, and unless you have a hired gun or somebody that knows the retail community sharing your market strengths to the national level retailers and restaurants specifically in the smaller, more rural markets, your community is probably not even being considered. When we started our company the first market analysis reports and demographic data we produced were incredibly complex. In total it was about 180-220 pages of information. We used this approach for about five years until a tenant rep broker from Chicago stopped me in Las Vegas and said "Rickey, I appreciate you sharing this with me" and then very respectfully let me know that he didn't have the time to go through all that information to compare his own tenant's data to our market reports. So the next year I invited a dozen of the nation's best tenant representatives to dinner in Las Vegas, fed them and poured a large quantity of alcohol down them. At the end of a two and half hour meal, I stood up and thanked them all for coming. Then I shared with them that the real reason that I asked them to come was to find out exactly what they needed to see about a potential market to allow them to feel comfortable about a new site for their respective tenant clients. All twelve agreed that there were only a few needed pieces of information, and that if I would cover those seven or eight categories of data they could let me know quickly if their tenants saw potential in that market. So armed with that information I came back to the office and completely reworked our market reports. Now we take data from six subscription data services in excel format, run the data through a proprietary HTML coding sequence, and produce market data that tenants and their broker reps, developers, and the public sector staff can access and compare very quickly. This has resulted in new retail deals in every community we have worked in that has stayed the course and embraced the long and grueling process of the development cycle.

There are reasons why people do not trust the government. Some are valid reasons and some are stupid reasons. In reality the public sector owes the taxpaying citizens, the local business community, and the consumers who come to the community to shop three things: transparency, accessibility, and financial responsibility. All citizens have an expectancy of safety, the right to privacy, and that the public sector is open to them and their needs. The public forum should always be a place where people can discuss and debate issues. Elected officials and city staff should always be approachable, respectful, and open to criticism. If more cities were open and responsive to public comments, those cowards on social media who won't come out in public, but who hide in darkness and spew their unwanted opinions wouldn't have the power to cause the chaos they cause. Fake news and made up reality should be a crime, and those who promulgate those lies should be held accountable. And you may not agree with what I am about to say, but you can be wrong if you want to be. If you are not willing to be a part of the "fixing" of the issue, you have no right to be complaining.

I shared about the damage that comes out of politics, and poor communication, and ignorance in the chapter on tension. I took a chapter to convey that all development of any kind takes longer than anyone is prepared to allow, and that it takes great patience and diligence, and tenacity to see deals through the process. I want to close this chapter on the differences between the public sector and the private sector by focusing on one more issue that will delay, kill, or destroy a deal faster than any other issue.

Competition is more heated between cities than ever before. The process of retail development is more competitive than ever before. Just in the past couple of years I have seen multiple developers fighting over a small number of tenants who had expressed interest in markets of similar population in cities our company has worked in. There has always been a rivalry and a struggle to get the right real estate or site for a tenant. The developer who was fortunate to get the site usually won the deal. In smaller markets, the obvious issue is that the real estate opportunities are very limited. What complicates the development of retail product even more is that when private landowners hear from interest from enough people, sometimes the greed factor kicks in and then the deals get really complicated. These deals all had a similar make-up. There were one or two big anchor tenants, and a lineup of smaller junior anchor and shadow tenants, and what all developers were looking for was a site where there was sufficient dirt to handle the deal and then a few pad sites out front where they could really make a decent return. As I said, in the smaller markets the availability of good sites diminishes very quickly. Another thing you can count on, especially in small or micropolitan markets is that word will eventually get out that retailers are looking and then the social media starts heating up and the next thing you know the rumor mill has created a mess.

So, one of the enemies of development in every setting, large or small, one tenant or a million square feet of tenants, is when the cat gets out of the bag before the cat herders can gain control again. I preach a few things in every community we work in. One is everyone needs to be engaged and pulling the same way. Another thing is that the city needs to be alert and responsive to the needs of the private sector. Along with these considerations, it will take longer to get it done than you are prepared for.

And last but not least, the public sector CANNOT talk about or discuss the deal at all. Not with their wives, or husbands, not with their friends, or the news media. Especially with the news media.

I do not want to give the impression that I am against the press. The press certainly has its place. I believe that the news media has a place in the free world and they certainly have a job to do. I believe personally that their job is to report the truth, the whole truth, and nothing but the truth. But let me assure you of one thing I know without a doubt. There are people in our society who cannot take the truth. You know I am right. There are segments of the general public that will not, or simply cannot handle the truth. The modern news media as we know it today is a biased mess. Right now people simply cannot count on getting the unbiased truth from the media. Social media and the internet is saturated with false and misleading "facts" that cannot be trusted and relied upon.

In a past life I worked for a decade and a half as a police officer. I learned very quickly on the street that truth in itself always has two sides. He says this, she says that. They both were involved in the same incident and both took their place on polar opposites sides of the "truth". He saw it one way, she saw it a completely different version of the same reality.

When you are reading the newspaper or watching news on television you are getting the "truth" from an individual whose perspective is always slanted one way or the other to say the least. And that slant may be more sinister than anything we have ever imagined. It seems that everyone has an agenda. No doubt the United States of America is the best country in the world. I sincerely believe that. But our country is messed up. It's messed up at the federal level, it's messed up at the state level, and I am fairly sure it's messed up in most local areas as well. At the local level, in the theatre of our daily lives, things could be better.

While development deals are being put together it is always prudent to keep the details below the radar.

If you have worked in the public sector at all, you know that there are certain rules municipalities have to abide by. Meetings are usually "open" meetings, meaning that an agenda is posted and the items being discussed are briefly described and the general public is invited to come see local government at work. But there are allowances designed to allow the discussion of certain sensitive topics with what is called an "executive session". Executive sessions are allowed to give the city administrators and elected officials the opportunity to discuss items involving public sector human resources items, litigation, and last but certainly not least, economic development issues. It is always prudent to keep development discussions while the deals are being put together private. Developers and retailers and restaurant tenants desire to keep the deals under the radar until real estate deals are being negotiated and contracted, public / private development agreements are being negotiated, and regulatory and development issues are being discussed and worked out. There are obvious reasons why this is a wise thing to do. For one thing land prices tend to get out of hand when the story gets out that commercial real estate is being looked at by the private sector. Also retailers and restaurant brands certainly do not want their competitors to know what they are doing. This is just good business. Surely anybody with just a little common sense can understand that. So let me touch on this very sensitive area of confidentiality one more time in closing. I personally like to have all city staff involved in development discussions, the city attorney, city manager, mayor and council, and anyone else involved from the public sector, sign non-disclosure agreements (NDAs) very early in the process of a retail deal, or for that matter, in any economic development project. Confidentiality agreements or NDAs usually outline the areas of confidentiality, the time frame no discussion is allowed, and make no mistake about it, if you violate an NDA on the public sector side you have just opened yourself, and the governmental entity you represent up to litigation. It is not uncommon for public sector entities to give projects pseudonyms to keep the project cloaked to protect the identity of those involved until the time is appropriate for announcing the finished project. There are good reasons why discretion is allowed. The problem is that my level of discretion may be completely different from your level of discretion.

Our company has worked directly or indirectly in over 440 cities. I have seen every type of municipal government operation that exists. It is always a pleasure for me to watch committed elected officials and city staff look at every agenda item and make their vote representative of what is the best consideration for the overall good of the public they were elected and hired to represent. I have encountered extremely intelligent city councils, and equally intelligent city managers and staffs. But I have also ran into some of the most ignorant, uneducated, unqualified, unscrupulous individuals on God's green earth in places of power in public sector settings. In the private sector, these type of individuals simply don't work out very well. In the private sector if you are ill-equipped, you get replaced. It always scares the bejesus out of me to see less than qualified people in the public setting flippantly making decisions that involve millions of dollars, and it ought to frighten you as well.

Common sense, discretion, and the ability to keep confidential information confidential should be required attributes for those who work in the public setting. In the private sector these same qualifications are needed as well. Most experienced developers, brokers, and the engineers and architects who plan development sites and work in the development business must be able to keep these deals under wraps.

In my humble opinion and due to the fact that I have seen with my own eyes what happens when people talk too much, I always chuckle when I see a broker, a landowner, a developer, or a city announce a deal before its done. It has been my experience that about 95% of these announcements don't ever turn into a real deal. When construction starts, concrete is being poured, steel is going up, it's usually ok to talk. But not before.

*[Thanks to the University of San Francisco Master of Public Administration Degree description for the idea for this chapter.]

CHAPTER 5

COMMON RETAIL DEVELOPMENT TERMINOLOGY FOR THE PUBLIC SECTOR

We have compiled a list of common terminology used by the private sector in development deals. This is not an exhaustive list but a lexicon of terms to help city staff, administrators, and elected officials understand and be better equipped to discuss and define ways to make the development process more efficient.

The following pages contain a collection of terms and concepts most commonly used in the commercial development of land and buildings. There are references to terms common in industrial, manufacturing, office, and retail development. Some terms apply across all the above sections and some are particular to the type of development discussed.

Abatement: Technically the interruption in the intensity or amount of something. In development terms it could mean many things. For example a landlord or developer may offer a tenant free or reduced rent for a fixed period of time. A city or governmental jurisdiction may offer an incentive in the form of tax abatements or discounts for a period of time. Also can be a requirement in certain development settings where the tenant or developer may be required to abate asbestos, noise, traffic or other restrictions to meet city codes, etc.

Absolute Net: Lease requiring tenant to pay in addition to base rent all costs associated with the operation, repair, & maintenance of the building, all real estate taxes & utilities, including repair & maintenance of the buildings structure and roof. Often the tenant is directly responsible, both for all such costs, and for the active handling of the items themselves.

Accelerator: A programming-based workplace designed to help startup companies grow more rapidly by providing them with technical and educational assistance, mentoring, networking opportunities and workspace.

**Adaptive
Reuse:** A building converted to a different use in order to meet current demand. Examples include a factory converted to retail use or an office building converted to a school.

Air Rights: A type of property interest referring to the "space" above land.

**Allowance or
Construction
Allowance:** The contribution by a landlord for the cost of tenant improvements in excess of the base building shell, often expressed as a cost per square foot with maximum amount stated.

Anchor: The major or prime tenant in a shopping center, mall, or free standing or in-line development. Also known as the "draw tenant", "anchor tenant", or "key tenant". An anchor is usually the largest, if not one of the largest store in a mall or shopping center. The anchor is usually a well-known department store or retail chain. Anchors benefit smaller or medium sized tenants by drawing in consumer traffic and increasing sales of the entire development. Larger shopping centers may have more than one anchor tenant. Rent for anchor tenants is often significantly lower than rent for other tenants in a shopping center because they draw consumers to the center.

Anchored: Indicates a shopping center with at least one major tenant already in business

Apron: The area, within the truck court, where trucks are parked for loading & unloading. This area will be paved with more durable material than will the rest of the truck court (e.g., concrete or other structural reinforcement vs. asphalt) to withstand the heavy loads being parked there.

As Is Condition: The acceptance by the tenant or buyer of the existing condition of real estate or building premises at the time the deal is closed or lease signing is consummated, including any defects.

Asking Rent: Amount asked by landlords for available space, expressed in dollars per square foot per year in most parts of the country (and per month in areas of California & other selected markets). (Synonym: face rate)

Assignment: Transfer by the lessee, [could be developer, owner, etc.] of lessee's entire estate of the property. This is distinguishable from a sublease where the sub lessee acquires something less than the lessee's entire interest.

Assessor's Parcel Number (APN): Number assigned to parcels of real property by the tax assessor of a particular jurisdiction for purposes of identification & record-keeping. It's unique within the particular jurisdiction, & may conform to certain formatting standards that convey basic identifying information such as the property type or location within the plat map.

Attorn: A tenant's agreement to recognize a new owner (including a foreclosing lender) as the new landlord, pay rent, & perform under the existing lease. To consent to the transfer of a rent or reversion. A tenant is said to attorn when he agrees to become the tenant of the person to whom the reversion has been granted.

Automobile Parking Ratio: Ratio calculated by comparing the number of parking spaces at a project to the gross leasable area (GLA) of a building. Usually expressed in number of spaces per 1,000 square feet of gross leasable space. It varies by property use, with labor-intensive operations needing higher parking ratios. For example, a building with a GLA of 800,000 sf would have 800 spaces expressed as 8 spaces/ 1,000 sf.

Available Space: Total amount of space that is currently being marketed for lease. It includes space that is vacant or space that is currently occupied but will be vacant in the future. Available space can include both direct & sublet space. If sublet space is excluded from the calculation, the term "direct available space" is recommended.

Augmented Reality: Augmented Reality (AR) is a concept that is just coming into its own in the modern retail world. In essence augmented reality is the morphing of computer generated objects into the real world and is becoming popular as retailers market their products via advertising on modern media. It includes shoppable catalogs, apps that let customers see instore deals when you point your phone's camera toward a specific item or as your computer mouse is clicked on a specific item in an online catalog to see the article move or allow the consumer to see the item from all sides.

B

Base rent: Set amount used as a minimum rent in a lease with provisions for increasing the rent over the term of the lease. The minimum rent due the landlord. Typically a fixed amount. It is a face, quoted, contract amount of periodic rent. The annual base rate is the amount on which escalations are calculated.

Base Year: In full service or modified gross leases, the landlord agrees to cover a tenant's share of the annual operating expenses, but limits their annual exposure to an amount equal to the expenses incurred in the first year, or "base year."

Basis Points (BPs): Values equal to one-hundredth of one percentage point. For example, 100 basis points = 1 percentage point.

Bay Depth: The distance between columns. (Synonyms: clear span, column spacing)

Bay Width: The distance from one side of the bay to the other

Beacons: Devices that are powered by BLE (Bluetooth Low Energy technology) & transmit messages to other blue tooth-enabled devices, such as smart phones, tablets, & computers. Beacons have the ability to recognize devices based on locations or previous interactions. This enables retailers to send tailored notifications to shoppers depending on where they are in the store or what classification of customer they are. For example a returning customer walks in, the store's beacon can send a "welcome back" message or if the shopper walks into a certain area of the store send a smart phone alert about a sale item. Beacons can also be used for in-store analytics purposes. Most of these are purposed designs to measure foot traffic, or dwell time in a certain area of the store, enabling retailers to gather data on their consumers and customers.

Big Box: A large establishment (often a square or rectangular shaped building) that is usually associated with a major retail chain or brand. Examples are Walmart, Target, Home Depot & Lowe's. These spaces can be back-filled with multiple tenants if the space is vacated by the original big box user.

Biotech Space: Highly specialized laboratory or research & development space uniquely configured & is typically developed to the needs of the biotech tenant. It may require significant retrofit should the tenant vacate the space. It is often characterized by robust mechanical, electrical & plumbing systems, as well as by sophisticated ventilation systems to accommodate the highly specialized & complex activities that occur inside and that involve the handling of chemicals, drugs and biological matter.

Blend & Extend: Lease type of renewal that allows tenants to blend their existing lease into a new and longer lease. If a tenant is paying rent that's above current market rents, this will lower the current rental rate. The tenant benefits by an immediate reduction in the rental rate, & the landlord benefits by securing a tenant for a longer term. Conversely, if rents are rising quickly & lease expiration is approaching a tenant may renew early & extend to lock in lower rates.

Breakpoint: Point at which an additional lease rate kicks in. For example, in addition to base rent, after a certain amount of sales revenue is generated in a month, a retailer will pay the landlord a percentage of in-store sales, typically 5%.

Brick and Click: Refers to retailers that integrate their brick & mortar store with their e-commerce site. They bring the best of both worlds into their business. Most brick & click companies even offer seamless web-to-store services such as instore pick up and returns.

Brownfield: Abandoned, idled, or underused land or facilities where expansion or redevelopment is complicated by real or perceived environmental contamination.

Building Classifications: Usually refer to Class A, B, C (sometimes D) properties. Classifications are subjective, Class A buildings generally feature superior construction & finish and are well located. They frequently offer covered parking. These buildings command the highest rental rates in their sub-market. The lower classes of buildings are progressively less desirable due to age, location or construction. Rents decline as the class of the property declines.

Building Code: Various laws, codes, & regulations set forth by the municipality with jurisdiction as to the end use of a piece of property & that dictate the criteria for design, use, materials, & types of improvements allowed.

Building or "Core Factor": Represents the percentage of net rentable square feet devoted to the building's common areas (lobbies, rest rooms, corridors, etc.). Can be computed for an entire building or a single floor. Also known as a loss factor or Rentable/Usable (R/U) factor, it is calculated by dividing the rentable square footage by the usable square footage.

Building Standard: List of construction materials & finishes that represent what the tenant improvement (finish) allowance/work letter is designed to cover while also serving to establish the landlord's minimum quality standards with respect to tenant finish improvements within the building. Examples are type & style of doors, lineal feet of partitions, quantity of lights, quality of floor covering, etc.

Building Standard plus Allowance: The landlord lists, in detail, the building standard materials & costs necessary to make the premises suitable for occupancy. A negotiated allowance is then provided for the tenant to customize or upgrade materials.

Build Out: The space improvements put in place per the tenants specifications. Build out takes into consideration the amount of tenant finish allowance provided for in the lease agreement.

Build to Suit: A way of leasing property, usually for commercial purposes, in which the developer or landlord builds to a tenant's specifications. The landowner pays for the construction to the specifications of the tenant, and the tenant then leases the land & building from the landowner, who retains ownership. A building is designed & tailored for a specific tenant, often because the tenant is unable to find suitable space in the speculative market. Sometimes a build-to-suit project includes specific design features not commonly found in the speculative market, thus compelling the tenant to have a special facility built. The build-to-suit project is usually contracted with a developer who owns & operates the completed facility occupied by the tenant. Generally, a build-to-suit project becomes a single-tenant building upon completion.

Buy Online and Pick Up In Store (BOPIS):
See Omni-channel retail

Buy Online and Return In Store (BORIS):
See Omni-channel retail

C

Cantilever Rack: Racking system containing shelving supports that are connected to vertical supports at the rear of the rack. This type of rack is used for storing long material such as lumber and piping.

Capital Expense or Cap Ex: An amount spent to acquire or improve a long-term asset such as equipment or buildings. Usually the cost is recorded in an account classified as Property, Plant and Equipment defined by reference to generally excepted accounting principles (GAAP). The cost (except for the cost of land) will be charged to depreciation expense over the useful life of the asset. Improvements (as opposed to repairs) to a fixed asset that will increase the value or useful life of that asset. A capital expenditure is typically amortized or depreciated over the useful life of the asset, as opposed to a repair, which is expensed in the year incurred.

**Capitalization Rate
or Cap Rate:** Unlevered initial return from the acquisition of a real estate asset calculated by dividing net operating income (NOI) by the property sales price. For example, a property's cap rate is 10% if it is purchased for $10 million and produces $1 million in NOI during one year. The cap rate is typically calculated using the NOI generated in the first year of ownership so investors can normalize and compare potential returns among competing investment properties.

Cashwrap: The main check out area of a retail store where shoppers go when they're ready to pay. It's where merchants set up their POS systems and ring up sales. Most cashwraps have shelves containing merchandise that can be added to the purchase on the way out.

Ceiling Height: Distance from the floor to the inside overhead upper surface of the room. This measure will be higher than any hanging objects, beams, joists or trusses, unless there is a suspended ceiling.

Certificate of Occupancy: Document presented by a local government agency or building department certifying that a building and/or the leased premises (tenant's space), has been satisfactorily inspected and is/are in a condition suitable for occupancy.

Class A Building: Classification used to describe an office building with rents in the top 30-40% of the marketplace. Class A buildings are well-located in major employment centers & typically have good transit, vehicular & pedestrian access. They are located adjacent to or in proximity to a high number of retail establishments & business-oriented or fast casual restaurants. Building services are characterized by above-average upkeep & management.

Class B Building: Classification used to describe an office building with rents that are based between those of Class A & C buildings. Class B buildings are in good to fair locations in major employment centers & have good to fair transit, vehicular & pedestrian access. They are located adjacent to or in proximity to a moderate number of retail establishments & business oriented or fast casual restaurants. Building services are characterized by average upkeep & management.

Class C Building: Classification used to describe an office building with rents in the bottom 10-20% of the marketplace. Class C buildings are in less-desirable locations relative to the needs of major tenant sectors in the marketplace. They can be older, neglected buildings in good locations or moderate-level buildings in poor locations, so transit, vehicular and pedestrian access may vary. Typically, fewer amenities & restaurants are found in or near these buildings, and they are usually of moderate to low quality. Building services are characterized by below-average upkeep & management.

Clear Height: Distance from the floor to the lowest hanging ceiling member or hanging objects, beams, joists or truss work descending down into a substantial portion of the industrial work area. The most important measure of the interior height of an industrial building because it defines the minimum height of usable space within the structure. (Synonyms: clear headway, clearance)

Clear Span: An open area with no obstructions.

Clear Span Facility: Building, most often a warehouse or parking garage, with vertical columns on the outside edges of the structure & a clear span between columns.

Click and Collect: Service in which retailers enable shoppers to buy items online & pick up in a brick & mortar store. Very popular with consumers because of convenience & no waiting or shipping of typical online purchases.

Clienteling: Technique used by retail associates to deepen their relationships with customers. They use CRM (customer relationship management) software to collect & track data, provide more personalized shopping experiences & follow up in a timely manner.

Column Spacing: Distance between posts or vertical supporting beams in a building

Common Area: There are two components of the term common area. If referred to in association with the rentable / usable or load factor calculation, the common areas are those areas within a building available for common use by all tenants or groups of tenants & their invitees (lobbies, corridors, restrooms). The cost of maintaining parking facilities, malls, sidewalks, landscaped areas, public toilets, truck & service facilities are included in the common area when calculating the tenant's pro-rata share of building operating expenses. The generally accessible areas found on each floor of the building such as washrooms, janitorial closets, electrical, mechanical & phone rooms, elevator lobbies & public corridors that are available for use by all tenants on that floor. It doesn't include major vertical penetrations such as elevator shafts, stairs, equipment runs, (a percentage of rentable area).

Commercial Mortgage-backed Securities (CMBS): Type of bond that is commonly issued in U.S. securities markets & is backed by the cash flow from a pool of mortgages on commercial properties. The CMBS are often arranged into groups or "tranches" according to geography, property type or underlying credit rating.

Common Area Maintenance (CAM): Additional rent charged to the tenant, in addition to base rent, to maintain the common areas of the property shared by the tenants & from which all benefit. Examples: snow removal, outdoor lighting, parking lot sweeping, insurance, property taxes, etc. Most often, this does not include any capital improvements (see "Capital Expenses") that are made to the property.

Community Center or
Community Shopping Center: A retail property with a wide range of apparel and general merchandise stores, as well as discount retailers or department stores such as Walmart, Kmart and Target.

Comparables or
Fair Market Comparables: Sometimes called "comps" lease rates and terms of properties similar in size, construction quality, age, use, and typically located within the same sub-market and used as comparison properties to determine the fair market lease rate for another property with similar characteristics. Refers to real estate pricing as well.

Competitive
Inventory: Single-tenant & multi-tenant buildings typically consist of 10,000 square feet or more that are owned by one party & are made available for lease to another party. Owner-occupied & government-owned buildings are typically excluded from the competitive inventory. Data providers each have their own set of buildings that make up the competitive inventory in their foundational data set. Some include buildings larger than 20,000 square feet, while others include buildings as small as 5,000 square feet. Those differences in the competitive set can cause variations in metrics such as vacancy & absorption reported by each.

Competitive
Set: Subset of total inventory that enables one to isolate & compare buildings on the basis of similar characteristics rather than by location. For example, a broker preparing to show available space to a tenant may identify five properties on the basis of location, square footage, class, asking rent & parking ratio. An investment sales or finance broker may generate a competitive set of buildings according to access to transit, year built & percentage leased to help estimate the value of an asset to be bought, sold or refinanced.

Concessions: Cash or equivalents expended by the landlord in the form of rental abatement, additional tenant finish allowance, moving expenses, cabling expenses or other monies expended to influence or persuade the tenant to sign a lease. To secure a tenant when vacancy is high in a market or submarket, a landlord may need to grant concessions in the lease. Concessions most often take the form of free rent but may also include lease buyouts, moving allowances & above-market tenant improvement allowances.

Condemnation: Process of taking private property, without the consent of the owner, by a governmental agency for public use through the power of eminent domain.

Construction Management: The construction process is overseen by a qualified construction manager who ensures that the various stages of are completed in a timely & seamless fashion, from getting the permit to completion of construction to the final walk-through of the completed leased premises with the tenant.

143

Consumer Price Index (CPI):

Measures inflation in relation to the change in the price of a fixed market basket of goods & services purchased by a specified population during a "base" period of time. It is not a true "cost of living" factor & bears little direct relation to actual costs of building operation or the value of real estate. The CPI is commonly used to increase the base rental periodically as a means of protecting the landlord's rental stream against inflation or to provide a cushion for operating expense increases for a landlord unwilling to undertake the record keeping necessary for operating expense escalations.

Contactless Payments:

Refers to a system of payments powered by near field communications (NFC). They include NFC-enabled credit and debit cards, smart cards, and smartphones that allow customers to complete transactions without physically touching a payment terminal. Instead of having to swipe their card, consumers can pay for their purchases by just waving their card or phone over a terminal.

Contiguous Space: (1) Multiple suites/spaces within the same building and on the same floor which can be combined and rented to a single tenant. (2) A block of space located on multiple adjoining floors in a building (i.e., a tenant leases floors 6 through 12 in a building)

Contiguous Block (s): Multiple suites or spaces on either the same floor or the adjoining floor(s) in the same building.

Contract Documents: Complete set of design plans & specifications for the construction of a building or of a building's interior improvements. Working drawings specify for the contractor the precise manner in which a project is to be constructed.

Contract Rent: Rental rates stipulated in an executed lease agreement. Typically, the contract rate is based on the first year rate as opposed to the average rate over the term of the lease. (Synonym: base rate)

145

Construction Starts: Total number of buildings that broke ground (commenced construction) over a given period. They are typically measured in number of buildings & square feet.

Convenience Store (C-Store): Retail store that carries a limited selection of basic items, as packaged foods and drugstore items which is open long hours for the convenience of shoppers. Usually with fuel sales and prepared foods.

Conversion: A building that is changed from one use to another (i.e., an office building that is converted to a multifamily building). Space being converted is removed from current inventory and included in the under construction category for the planned future use (i.e., an office building being converted to an apartment building will be removed from office inventory and included under apartment space, or number of units, under construction).

Core Area: Common area plus vertical penetrations in an office building measured in square feet. It is typically expressed as a percentage of net rentable area. This factor, which ranges from 5% to 20% for typical office buildings, can be computed for an entire building or a single floor.

Core Factor: Represents the percentage of net rentable square feet devoted to the building's common areas (lobbies, restrooms, corridors, etc.). This factor can be computed for an entire building or a single floor. Also known as a loss factor or rentable/usable (R/U) factor, it is calculated by dividing the rentable square footage by the usable square footage.

Core Investment: An investment in a high-quality real estate asset that is located in a highly accessible and highly desirable submarket. The asset commands among that submarket's highest rents and requires virtually zero near-term capital expenditures. The asset is at least 80 percent leased, carries long-term leases with creditworthy tenants, and is among the most sought-after assets in the market, suggesting there is significant market liquidity.

Co-tenancy: A clause in a retail tenant's lease that provides remedies to a tenant in the event that another tenant, typically an anchor or major tenant, ceases its operations at the property.

Covenant: A written agreement inserted into deeds or other legal instruments stipulating performance or non-performance of certain acts or, uses or non-use of a property and/or land.

Covenant of Quiet Enjoyment: The old "quiet enjoyment" paragraph, now more commonly referred to as "Warranty of Possession", had nothing to do with noise in and around the leased premises. It provides a warranty by landlord that it has the legal ability to convey the possession of the premises to tenant; the landlord doesn't warrant that he owns the land. This is the essence of the landlord's agreement & the tenant's obligation to pay rent. If the landlord breaches this warranty, it constitutes an actual or constructive eviction.

Co-Working Space: Workspace offered for lease for short- to long-term periods in a communal setting. Space for office, artistic or manufacturing use can be leased by the day, month, year or even hour. The physical space leased can range from a traditional dedicated private office with a door to an unassigned seat on a bench along a communal table. Co-working spaces go beyond just providing a physical work environment. They are typically operated by entities that offer business-related lectures, social events & a sense of community for their entrepreneurial tenants, thus helping them grow their businesses.

Creative Office Space: Previously industrial space with high ceilings and exposed air ducts. The space is often made of brick and timber and has been converted to office or studio space that often caters to technology, advertising, media and entertainment tenants (TAME).

**Creditworthy
Tenant**: Tenant with a business that has been in existence for numerous years, that has strong financial statements, or has a large market presence that could be rated as investment grade by a rating agency. Financial & business stability implies that the tenant is highly likely to honor its lease commitment; and is, therefore, viewed as a low-risk renter. Buildings with credit tenants as anchors are considered less risky investments for lenders.

Cross Dock: Loading docks on opposite sides of a relatively shallow distribution facility that allow for quick loading, sorting or unloading from one vehicle to another.

Cubic Volume: In many industrial facilities, the cubic volume of the building must be calculated so a user can determine the size and type of racking and sorting equipment that can be accommodated.

Cure: A term in real estate that allows a time period (usually specified in the contract) for any situation arising that may cause a breach in the contract for either party.

D

Dead Stock: Retailers nightmare. Also called dead inventory, it pertains to merchandise that has never been sold or has been in stock for a while. Sometimes it's because an item is seasonal, or worst case scenario it isn't popular or in demand.

Debt Coverage Ratio: The ratio of the net operating income to the mortgage payment. If net operating income is projected to change over time, the investor typically reports the first year's net operating income.

Default: General failure to perform a legal or contractual duty under a commercial lease, such as not paying rent when due, or the breach of other nonmonetary lease covenants.

Delivered: Building that has completed construction (obtained its certificate of occupancy). With a COO, the property will be considered delivered whether or not tenants have occupied the space.

Delivered Premises Definitions:
Vanilla Shell:
In most cases the landlord will provide a "vanilla shell" or some modified version thereof. Sometimes referred to as a "white box" because of the installation of a white dropped ceiling and white sheet-rocked walls. A vanilla shell build out typically includes:

- One restroom to code in a location designated by landlord, typically at the rear of premises
- Sheet-rocked, taped and painted walls (painting negotiable)
- Concrete floor slab, broom swept
- Suspended, dropped t-bar ceiling usually with a 2' x 4' grid
- 200-400 amp low voltage electrical service distributed per code
- Fluorescent 4' x 2' lighting fixtures with usually one fixture per 150-200 square feet
- HVAC distributed at one ton per 300-350 square feet depending upon local climate conditions and use (restaurants require more than retail). Heating is usually a gas system and air conditioning is electrical
- Fire sprinklers per code distributed throughout the space based upon retail use
- Water, gas, cable and telephone service stubbed to the rear of the premises

Above standard improvements:
There is a wide range of "above-standard" tenant improvements that tenants may request. The space can be described as "turnkey" if the space is fully built out for the tenant short of furniture; fixtures and equipment. The above-standard improvements that tenants typically request are:

> Floor covering – carpet, tile or wood
> Special wall finishes such as special painting, wall coverings or wood paneling
> Additional plumbing and/or electrical capacity and distribution, especially for restaurants or hair salons
> Upgraded lighting fixtures such as 2' x 2' fixtures or trac or recessed lighting
> A second restroom, especially for restaurants (who will be required to install two restrooms in most cases)
> Above-standard HVAC, especially for restaurants or those tenants that have a high electrical load for lighting fixtures, electronics or computers
> Grease traps for restaurants
> Upgraded kitchen fire sprinkler systems or vented hood exhaust systems for restaurants
> Demising walls for dressing rooms; storage or office areas
> Cabinetry or cash register "cash wrap" stations;
> Additional entry doors or automatic electric doors
> Upgraded storefront treatments

Cold dark shell:
The Landlord builds the shell & delivers to the tenant a concrete floor slab, exterior walls, roof, storefront & electric (w/o panel), gas, water & sewer services stubbed to the premises.

➢ Tenant installs HVAC & distributes within the space.
➢ Fire sprinklers to meet shell building code and installed with the shell.

Warm gray shell:
The landlord provides the cold, dark shell condition plus installs an electrical panel (with breakers) & an HVAC unit, but does not distribute the electrical or HVAC service within the space.

Demising Walls: The partition wall that separates one tenant's space from another space or from the building's common area, such as a hallway.

Design Build: System in which a single entity is responsible for both the design & construction. Can apply to an entire facility or to individual components of the construction to be performed by a subcontractor; also referred to as "design/construct".

Depreciation: Spreading out the cost of a capital asset over its estimated useful life or a decrease in the usefulness, & therefore value, of real property improvements or other assets caused by deterioration or obsolescence.

Discount Rate: Interest rate used in discounted cash flow (DCF) analysis to determine the present value of future cash flows.

Distraint: Act of seizing (legally or illegally) personal property based on the right and interest which a landlord has in the property of a tenant in default.

Distribution Building: Type of warehouse facility designed to accommodate efficient movement of goods.

Direct New Space: Space offered for lease directly by the building owner or landlord. If space is offered for lease by a building tenant, it's not direct space but rather is sublet space.

Direct Vacancy Rate: Total amount of physically vacant space divided by the total amount of existing inventory, expressed as a percentage. Space under construction (therefore vacant) isn't included in vacancy calculations.

Dock High Door: Loading dock door that is not at ground level but rather is elevated to 4 feet in order to be even with the standard tractor-trailer height for loading or unloading goods without a change in elevation. Some doors, called semidock or half dock, are constructed at a 2-foot height to accommodate smaller or lower delivery trucks.

Dollar or Expense Stop: An agreed dollar amount of taxes and operating expense (expressed for the building as a whole or on a square foot basis) over which the tenant will pay its prorated share of increases. May be applied to specific expenses (e.g., property taxes or insurance).

Door-to-square-foot ratio: The ratio of the total number of loading docks & drive-in doors to the building's total square feet

Drive In Door: Door through which trucks, forklifts, & other machinery or vehicles can enter & exit without a change in elevation.

Drive Time Approach: Approach to estimating the trade area (and sales/revenue potential) for a given retail establishment or center based on the central place theory concept of range & how far people are willing to travel to obtain retail goods as defined by drive time & mileage.

Drop Shipping: Arrangement between a retailer & a manufacturer or distributor in which the former transfers customer orders to the latter, who then ships the merchandise directly to the consumer. The retailer doesn't keep the products in stock, it sends the orders & shipment information to the manufacturer who ships directly to the consumer.

Drug Store: Store that sells medicines & various other products such as groceries, beer, wine, cards, all manner of health & beauty aids.

Dynamic Clustering: A tool used by modern retailers that targets & identifies patterns or opportunities in various & diverse segments across a wide demographic or geographic range. It enables the retailers to make more strategic sales, location, or marketing decisions.

E

E-Commerce: The buying & selling of products or services mostly through the internet. Typically, transactions are carried out via computers & mobile devices such as smartphones & tablets.

Effective Rent: Actual rental rate to be achieved by the landlord after deducting the value of concessions from the base rental rate paid by a tenant, usually expressed as an average rate over the term of the lease. Expressed in dollars per square foot either per year or per month depending on market standards, it's a measurement of the value of the lease when all the concessions plus escalations are included. Effective rent calculations may vary according to local market practices; for example, in some markets, broker commissions are included. The average per square foot rent paid by the tenant over the lease term. Takes into account only free rents and stepped rents. Doesn't include allowances, space pockets, free parking, or other similar landlord concessions.

Efficiency Factor: Represents the percentage of net rentable square feet devoted to the building's common areas (lobbies, rest rooms, corridors, etc.). It can be computed for an entire building or a single floor. Also known as a core factor or rentable/usable (R/U) factor, it is calculated by dividing the rentable square footage by the usable square footage.

Eminent Domain: Power of the state, municipalities, & private persons or corporations authorized to exercise functions of public character to acquire private property for public use by condemnation, in return for just compensation.

EMV: EMV was developed by Europay, Mastercard, & Visa, hence the name, as a way to combat fraud. It's a technology that powers chip-and-pin cards, a type of debit & credit cards that are far more secure than magnetic strip cards. Unlike the magnetic stripe card, which stores static information about the cardholder, an EMV card is embedded with a chip, which creates a unique code that changes for every transaction. Making it less susceptible to fraud because the original transaction code is not usable again & the card would automatically be declined.

Encroachment: The intrusion of a structure which extends, without permission, over a property line, easement boundary or building setback line.

Encumbered Space: A block of space offered for lease by a landlord to which another tenant has some right to lease or occupy at some future date.

Endless Aisle: A feature of brick-and-mortar stores that enables customers to browse & shop the retailer's entire catalog of products. Rather than stocking up on every item, they implement an endless aisle by giving shoppers access to touch screens. Nike is using endless aisles in their store in Pasadena, CA. Large touch screens enable customers to browse the entire inventory. If they see something they like, they can purchase it in-store and Nike will ship it to them.

Energy Star: Also referred to as an EPA rating or an Energy Star rating, it is a standardized national benchmark that helps architects & building owners assess energy use relative to similar buildings in the program. An Energy Star-qualified building means it meets EPA criteria for energy efficiency & displays the Energy Star building label.

Encumbrance: Any right to, or interest in, real property held by someone other than the owner, but which will not prevent the transfer of fee title (i.e. a claim, lien, charge or liability attached to and binding real property).

EPOS: Abbreviation for electronic point of sale. Computerized system used to record sales & control inventory.

Equity: Fair market value of an asset less any outstanding indebtedness or other encumbrances.

Escalation Clause: A clause in a lease which provides for the rent to be increased to reflect changes in expenses paid by the landlord such as real estate taxes, operating costs, etc. This may be accomplished by several means such as fixed periodic increases, increases tied to the consumer price index or adjustments based on changes in expenses paid by the landlord in relation to a dollar number per square foot or base year reference.

**Estoppel
Certificate**: Signed statement certifying that certain statements of fact are correct as of that date & can be relied upon by a third party, including a prospective lender or purchaser. In the context of a lease, a statement by a tenant identifying that the lease is in effect & certifying that no rent has been prepaid & that there are no known outstanding defaults by the landlord (except those specified).

**Exclusive Agency
Listing**: Written agreement between a real estate broker & a property owner in which the owner promises to pay a fee or commission to the broker if specified real estate property is leased during the listing period. The broker need not be the procuring cause of the lease.

Expansion Option: A right for the tenant to increase the size of its premises under specified terms & conditions. It's a right granted by the landlord to the tenant whereby the tenant has the option(s) to add more space to its premises pursuant to the terms of the options.

Expense Stop: An agreed dollar amount of taxes and operating expense (expressed for the building as a whole or on a square foot basis) over which the tenant will pay its prorated share of increases. May be applied to specific expenses (e.g. property taxes or insurance).

Experiential Retail: The notion that people buy goods online but pursue experiences at brick and-mortar locations (i.e., do yoga, eat at restaurants, visit flagship stores for experience and entertainment, etc.).

Extension Option: An agreed continuation of occupancy under the same conditions, as opposed to a renewal, which implies new terms or conditions to the lease. In a lease, it is a right granted by the landlord to the tenant whereby the tenant has an option to extend the lease for an additional period of time.

Exurban: An emerging residential area beyond built-up suburbs and edge cities.

F

Fair Market Rent: The rent which would normally be agreed upon by a willing landlord and tenant in an "arm's length transaction" for a specific property at a given time, even though the actual rent may be different. In a lease, the fair market rent is defined in a number of different ways and is subject to extensive negotiation and interpretation.

Fair Market Value: The sale price at which a property would change hands between a willing buyer and willing seller, neither being under any compulsion to buy or sell and both having reasonable knowledge of the relevant facts. Also known as FMV.

Features: Property characteristics that determine the market niche of the shopping center.

First Generation
Space: Generally refers to new space that is currently available for lease and has never before been occupied by a tenant. There are different kinds of this type of space. See delivered premises definition

First Mortgage: The senior mortgage which, by reason of its position, has priority over all junior encumbrances. The holder of the first/ senior mortgage has a priority right to payment in the event of default.

First Right
of Refusal: Lease clause giving a tenant the first opportunity to buy or lease a property at the same price & on the same terms & conditions as those contained in a third party offer that the owner has expressed a willingness to accept. Such rights often pertain to adjacent space. Also seen in other non-retail real estate transactions.

Fixed Lease: A lease in which the lessee pays a fixed rental amount for the duration of the lease.

Flash Sales: Closely related to daily deals, it refers to sale events that take place for a limited time. They can last anywhere from several hours to a couple of days & entice consumers with huge bargains (usually 50% and up). The catch is, shoppers have to complete the purchase ASAP. Otherwise, they risk losing the items to other shoppers or run out of time & miss the deals. Zulily, a shopping site for moms, babies & kids, is an example of a flash sale website. Events open at 6am PDT & usually last 72 hours (some are one-day sales). Then they scoot away to make room for new events. Customers are encouraged to shop early & fast, so they can get their hands on the widest selection. Zulily announces flash sales in advance so moms can prep for the sales they wish to attend.

Flex Space: A building providing its occupants the flexibility of utilizing the space with a configuration allowing a flexible amount of office or showroom space in combination with manufacturing, laboratory, warehouse distribution, etc. Can also provide the flexibility to relocate overhead doors. Generally constructed with little or no common areas, load-bearing floors, loading dock facilities & high ceilings.

Flex Facility: An industrial building designed to be used in a variety of ways. Usually located in an industrial park setting. Specialized flex buildings can include service centers, showrooms, offices, warehouses and more.

Floor Area Ratio: The ratio of the gross square footage of a building to the land on which it is situated. Calculated by dividing the total square footage in the building by the square footage of land area. FAR is the relationship between the total square footage of a building & the total square footage of the parcel on which the building is located. It is typically calculated by dividing the total square footage of the building by the land area in square feet. For example, if a 20,000-square-foot building is built on a 10,000-square-foot lot, the FAR is 2.0.

Floor Plate: The gross square footage of each floor in a multistory building. Individual floor plate sizes may vary according to the design of a building.

Force Majeure: A force that can't be controlled by the parties to a contract & prevents them from complying with the provisions of the contract. This includes acts of God such as a flood or hurricane or, acts of man such as a strike, fire or war.

Foreclosure: Procedure by which the mortgagee (lender) either takes title to or forces the sale of the mortgagor's (borrower) property in satisfaction of a debt.

Free Rent / Rent Concessions: Concession granted by a landlord to a tenant whereby the tenant is excused from paying rent for a slated period during the lease term.

Freestanding: A single-tenant property that is separate from a shopping center. Stand-alone retail structure that is not part of a complex (i.e., bank, bowling alley, Walmart).

Full Service Rent / Lease: All-inclusive rental rate that includes operating expenses & real estate taxes for the first year. The tenant is generally still responsible for increases in operating expenses over the base year amount. Same as a gross lease. Opposite of a net lease.

Fulfillment Center: An industrial property type that enables goods to be efficiently moved or transported from a warehouse directly to a consumer.

Functional Obsolescence: A descriptive term used to characterize a building that cannot be improved to meet current market standards or tastes without a complete replacement of buildings systems and finishes.

Future Proposed Space: Space in a proposed commercial development which is not yet under construction or where no construction start date has been set. Future proposed projects include all those projects waiting for a lead tenant, financing, zoning, approvals or any other event necessary to begin construction. Also may refer to the future phases of a multi-phase project not yet built.

G

Go Dark: A clause in a retail tenant's lease that allows a tenant to cease operations at a property if a defined event, such as the departure of an anchor tenant, should occur.

Government Office Building: Building owned & typically occupied by public sector entities.

Graduated Lease: Lease, generally long term, which provides that the rent will vary depending upon future contingencies, such as a periodic appraisal, the tenant's gross income or the passage of time.

Green Globes: Founded in Canada in 1996, Green Globes is a green building guidance & assessment program that offers a way to advance the environmental performance & sustainability of commercial buildings. After achieving a minimum of 350 of the possible 1,000 points, new & existing commercial buildings can be certified for their environmental achievements by pursuing a Green Globes certificate that assigns a rating of 1 to 4 globes.

Green Retailing: Refers to the environmentally-friendly practices that retailers get into. These can include switching a product's packaging to a recyclable one or giving customers reusable shopping bags instead of plastic. Other practices, such adding solar panels or replacing store lighting with energy-saving alternatives are also considered as green retailing.

Grocery: Retail store that sells food & other non-food items. Large grocery stores that stock products other than food, such as clothing or household items are called supermarkets.

Gross Absorption: Total amount of space occupied over a given period of time, without subtracting the amount of space vacated.

Gross Building Area: Total floor area of the building measuring from the outer surface of exterior walls & windows & including all vertical penetrations (e.g. elevator shafts) & basement space. Usually measured from the innermost edge of the outside walls.

Gross Lease: Lease in which the tenant pays a flat sum for rent out of which the landlord must pay all expenses such as taxes, insurance, maintenance & utilities. A legally binding contract in which a landlord receives stipulated rent from a tenant & is obligated to pay all or most of the property's operating expenses & real estate taxes. Note: Disclosure of the specified costs of operation is required in some states.

Gross Leasable Area (GLA): A site calculated as the summation of all rentable areas plus all common areas of a building.

Ground Lease: Lease agreement (contract) whereby the landowner (lessor) agrees to lease a parcel of land for a set period of time to a 3rd party (lessee). Depending on the agreement, the lessor can stipulate what the lessee can or can't do with the property or build on the property. The lease term is typically 20 years or more, but many extend to 99 years. Upon expiration of the agreement, the lessor typically gains control & ownership of whatever is constructed on the land, unless the lease is renewed or an exception is created in the lease. Rent paid to the owner for use of land, normally on which to build a building. Generally, the arrangement is that of a long-term lease (e.g., 99 years) with the lessor retaining title to the land. Also called ground rent.

Guarantor: One who makes a guaranty or promises to pay a third party's obligations.

Guaranty: Agreement whereby the guarantor undertakes collaterally to assure satisfaction of the debt of another or perform the obligation of another if and when the debtor fails to do so. Differs from a surety agreement in that there is a separate and distinct contract rather than a joint undertaking with the principal.

H

**High Speed
Retail:** Born out of people's need for faster services & less wait time, high speed retail is about making the customer's shopping experience much quicker. Examples can include drive-thru grocery stores, pop-up stores, mobile businesses such as food trucks, or any retailer that implements urgent promotions or limited-time sales. The use of mobile POS systems is extremely common in high speed retail. This is because aside from being fast, lightweight & easy to set up, mPOS solutions run in the cloud & can update every aspect of the business (inventory, CRM, payments, etc.) in real-time, helping merchants stay up-to-date at all times. Most mPOS systems have convenient capabilities like emailing receipts & processing mobile payments, making it easy for retailers to conduct business faster.

High Cube: A relative term that refers to industrial buildings with an abundance of clear height or vertical cubic space. (Synonym: high bay)

High Street Retail: A concentration of shops in urban or urban-like areas that may also be referred to as "Main Street retail" in the United States and Canada.

Hold Over Tenant: A tenant retaining possession of the leased premises after the expiration of a lease.

HVAC: The acronym for "Heating, Ventilating and Air-Conditioning". A general term encompassing any system designed to heat and cool a building in its entirety, as opposed to a space heater.

I

Improvements: Usually refers to the improvements made to or inside a building but may include any permanent structure or other development, like a street, sidewalks, utilities, etc.

Incentive: Anything a public sector entity can do to assist the private sector to alleviate risk, add public funds to a development deal to help pay for public infrastructure, to expedite or speed up a deal, etc.

Incubator: Economic development tool created to support new businesses. Typically lab or office space or both provided for free or at a deep discount in buildings owned or leased by municipalities. Business assistance and financing opportunities may be provided as startups gain momentum.

Industrial Building: Structure used for manufacturing, research & development, production, maintenance & storage or distribution of goods or both. Can include some office space. Industrial buildings are divided into 3 primary classifications: manufacturing, warehouse or distribution, & flex.

Infill: Development of one or more buildings on underutilized land situated between existing buildings. It is typically done in dense environments where land is scarce. The broader term land-recycling is sometimes used.

In-line space: A retail store placed adjacent to neighboring retailers so that the fronts of the stores are in a straight line & behind what is considered the lease line. Tenants operating in the common area are not considered in-line vendors.

Innovation Center or District: Geographic areas with concentrations of innovative firms & entrepreneurial activity that focus on strengthening & growing new businesses & commercializing their products or services or both.

Integrated Supply Chain: Network of businesses & contractors that work together to manufacture, transport, distribute, & sell retail goods. Unlike a regular supply chain which is more of a linear process that follows a product from one phase to the next, an integrated supply chain is more collaborative & can entail joint product development, shared information & common systems.

Internal Rate of Return: For income properties, it is the interest or discount rate needed to discount the sum of future net cash flows, including amortization and payments of loans & depreciation of the real property, to an amount equal to the initial equity of the property. For development projects, it is the interest or discount rate needed to convert (or discount or reduce) the sum of the development expenditures & incomes to equal zero.

Internet of Things (IoT): The concept of getting objects such as cars or household appliances to "talk" to each other. More things can now connect to the web, and this enables them to communicate with one another. Smartphones can connect to speakers, clocks, lamps, and more. Forward-thinking retailers are now using connected devices to streamline in-store shopping and communicate with shoppers.

J

Jerry-Built: Built cheaply or flimsily.

Jurisdiction: The power, right, or authority to interpret and apply the law, i.e. in zoning, annexation, or building codes; the limits or territory within which the authority may be exercised.

K

Keystone Pricing: This is the practice of selling merchandise at a rate that's double its wholesale price. Retailers use the keystone pricing formula because it's simple and it usually covers costs while providing a sound profit margin.

Kiosk: A small, physically independent stand or cart often placed within the common area of a retail structure (typically a regional mall) from which specialty goods are sold.

Knowledge: Understanding gained by actual experience; a clear perception of truth or reality; knowing how to do something smoothly or efficiently. [*I know you may shake your head at this definition, but in all seriousness, the public sector many times attempts to tackle issues with which they have no or very little knowledge. The solution in terms of economic development strategy, retail market analysis, retail recruiting, and other economic development issues is to hire a consultant or a consulting firm like Retail Attractions, LLC*]

L

Layaway / Lay-by: An agreement between the retailer & the customer in which the retailer puts an item on hold until it is paid for in full. The customer pays for in installments (interest-free), & will only receive the item once the payments are complete. The arrangement is a win for both parties. Layaway programs make it easier for customers to afford products they want, while minimizing risk for retailers.

Lease: An agreement whereby the owner of real property (i.e., landlord/ lessor) gives the right of possession to another (i.e., tenant/ lessee) for a specified period of time (i.e., term) and for a specified consideration (i.e., rent).

Lease Agreement: The formal legal document entered into between a landlord and a tenant to reflect the terms of the negotiations between them; that is, the lease terms have been negotiated and agreed upon, and the agreement has been reduced to writing. It constitutes the entire agreement between the parties and sets forth their basic legal rights.

Lease Commencement Date: The date usually constitutes the commencement of the term of the lease for all purposes, whether or not the tenant has actually taken possession so long as beneficial occupancy is possible. In reality, there could be other agreements, such as an early occupancy agreement, which have an impact on this strict definition.

Leasehold: An ownership structure in which a temporary right to use land has been granted by the landowner to another party. (See ground lease.) Although the tenants don't own the land, they are able to improve the land & operate it as stipulated in the ground lease for the term of the lease.

Leasehold Improvements: Improvements made to the leased premises by or for a tenant. Generally, especially in new space, part of the negotiations will include in some detail the improvements to be made in the leased premises by landlord.

Leased Space: Space under contract between a landlord & a tenant or between a tenant & a subtenant.

Leasing Activity: Refers to the number of leases signed or square footage committed to over a specified period without regard to occupancy. Typically, leases are executed many months before a tenant occupies the space. This arrangement means that a lease can be executed in a given quarter, but the space commitment will not show up in the absorption figures until the space is occupied. Leasing activity includes direct leases, subleases & expansions of existing leases. It also includes any preleasing activity in buildings that are under construction, are planned or are under renovation. (Synonym: gross absorption)

LEED: Leadership in Energy and Environmental Design (LEED) is a third-party certificate program under the U.S. Green Building Council (USGBC). A nationally accepted benchmark for the design, construction & operation of high-performance sustainable buildings. Certificate levels are: Certified, Silver, Gold or Platinum & are based on points obtained in 6 areas: sustainable sites, water efficiency, energy & atmosphere, material & resources, indoor environmental quality, & innovation in design.

Legal Description: Geographical description that identifies a parcel of land by government survey, metes and bounds, or lot numbers of a recorded plat including a description of any portion thereof that is subject to an easement or reservation.

Letter of Credit: Commitment by a bank or other person, made at the request of a customer, that the issuer will honor drafts or other demands for payment upon full compliance with the conditions specified in the letter. They are often used in place of cash deposited with the landlord to satisfy security deposit requirements.

Letter of Intent: Preliminary agreement stating the proposed terms for a final contract. They can be binding or non-binding. This is the threshold issue in most litigation concerning letters of intent. The parties should consult their respective legal counsel before signing any letter of intent. An agreement(s) between 2 or more parties before an actual agreement, such as a lease, is finalized. It's similar to a term sheet or memorandum of understanding (MOU). While LOIs may not be binding, provisions of them can be, e.g., non-disclosure & exclusivity. The intent is to protect both parties in the transaction until it is executed.

Less Than Truckload (LTL) Shipping: Transportation of lightweight freight or smaller groupings of freight. LTL shipments typically weigh between 151 & 20,000 lbs. LTL carriers collect freight from various shippers & consolidate it onto enclosed trailers for line haul (the movement of cargo between 2 major cities or ports) to the delivering terminal or to a hub terminal.

Leveler: Steel plates that are moved by auto-hydraulic lifts to make a loading dock level with a truck bed. A fully loaded truck may sit 4 to 6 inches lower than a standard 48-inch-high dock. The device is used to account for the difference so a forklift can be driven into and out of a truck. A building equipped with multiple loading docks may not have a leveler for each dock.

Leveraged Buy-Out: Purchase of a company using borrowed funds. The purchaser will use the company's assets as collateral so they can get the loan to buy it, & they will use the acquired company's cash flow (i.e. retail sales) to repay it.

Lien: A claim or encumbrance against property used to secure a debt, charge or the performance of some act. Includes liens acquired by contract or by operation of law. Note that all liens are encumbrances but all encumbrances are not liens.

Lien Waiver (Waiver of Liens): A waiver of mechanic's lien rights, signed by a general contractor & his subcontractors, that is often required before the general contractor can receive a draw under the payment provisions of a construction contract. May also be required before the owner can receive a draw on a construction loan.

Lifestyle Center: Upscale national-chain specialty stores usually in an outdoor setting. Type of retail property in an urban-like or Main Street setting with pedestrian circulation in the core with vehicular circulation along the perimeter. Tenants are upscale, national-chain specialty stores, restaurants & theaters. Note: while lifestyle centers have typical size guidelines (150,000 - 500,000sf), the size doesn't dictate its classification.

Listing Agreement: Agreement between the property owner & a real estate broker giving the broker authorization to sell or lease the property at a certain price & terms in return for a commission, set fee or other compensation.

**Load Factor
or Core Factor**: The load factor is calculated by dividing the rentable building area (RBA) by the usable area. This factor can then be applied to the usable area to convert it to RBA for comparison. In markets where space is leased on the basis of the usable area, if the load factor is 15%, then the usable area can be multiplied by 1.15, resulting in the RBA.

Loading Dock: An elevated platform at the shipping or delivery door of a building; usually situated at the same height as the floor of a shipping container on a truck or railroad car to facilitate loading & unloading. Loading docks can be exterior ramps that protrude from a building & are covered with a canopy or some element to protect the loading area from the elements. They can be flush with the exterior of the building & accessed through a sliding door adjacent to the interior of the building.

Loan To Value Ratio (LTV): The ratio between a mortgage loan and the value of the property pledged as security, usually expressed as a percentage.

Locker: Storage compartment that enables a purchaser to pick up merchandise at a convenient satellite location. This arrangement allows for a type of self-service parcel delivery. Customers can select any locker location as their delivery address and can retrieve orders at that location by entering a unique pickup code on the locker touchscreen.

Long Term Lease: In most markets, this refers to a lease whose term is at least three years from initial signing until the date of expiration or renewal option. [Can be five or ten years]

Lot: Generally, one of several contiguous parcels of land making up a fractional part or subdivision of a block, the boundaries of which are shown on recorded maps and "plats".

Loss Leader: A known marketing tool in retail, a loss leader is an item that's sold at a loss in order to attract more customers into a store. Once they're inside, the retailer counts on the customer to buy other things together with the loss leader, thus generating profits for the business.

Lump Sum Contract: A type of construction contract requiring the general contractor to complete a building or project for a fixed cost normally established by competitive bidding. The contractor absorbs any loss or retains any profit.

M

M-Commerce: Mobile commerce is buying & selling via non-tethered devices such as smartphones & tablets.

Mall & Other: "Mall" indicates that the shopping center is enclosed & the shop's entrances are predominantly facing the center's interior while "Other" indicates retail properties that are neither enclosed malls nor unenclosed strip centers/retail parks.

Manufacturing Building: Facility used for the conversion, fabrication or assembly of raw or partly wrought materials into products or goods.

Markdown: Unlike limited-time sales or promotional discounts, a markdown is a devaluation of a product due to its inability to be sold at the intended price. The price of the merchandise is permanently reduced to move inventory & make room for new products.

Market: In commercial real estate (CRE), the term "market" has many characteristics.

1. Hierarchy: In terms of geographic hierarchy, a region is made up of markets, & a market is made up of submarkets.

2. Boundaries: Markets & submarkets have generally accepted geographic boundaries that don't overlap. They are most commonly bound by streets, roads & natural features such as parks & rivers, which clearly indicate where one market or submarket ends & another begins.

3. Purpose: Markets & submarkets are the foundation upon which analysts track real estate fundamentals such as vacancy, absorption, rents & construction activity.

4. Markets & submarkets are further broken down by total buildings & by total square footage in those buildings.

5. Product types: Office & industrial product types may share generally accepted market or submarket boundaries because in the US, office space tends to be clustered together as does industrial space. However, there may also be separate & distinct boundaries for each respective property type. Suburban retail is more closely tied to residential and, therefore, is dispersed across large geographic areas, whereas urban retail is typically clustered in specific areas or on specific streets.

Market Rent: The rental income that a property would command on the open market with a landlord and a tenant ready and willing to consummate a lease in the ordinary course of business; indicated by the rents that landlords were willing to accept and tenants were willing to pay in recent lease transactions for comparable space.

Master Lease: A primary lease that controls subsequent leases and which may cover more property than subsequent leases. The controlling lease identifying the terms and length of the lease. Note that a sublease cannot extend beyond the term of the master lease. An executive suite operation is a good example in that a primary lease is signed with the landlord and then individual offices within the leased premises are leased to other individuals or companies.

Mass Customization: Author B. Joseph Pine II said it best: "Today I define mass customization as the low-cost, high-volume, efficient production of individually customized offerings." Mass customization refers to the practice of offering products that can be tailored to each person's preferences, but can still be produced with mass-production efficiency. Pine, in his Harvard Business Review piece entitled Beyond Mass Customization, advised businesses to take their offering & break it apart into modular elements, similar to LEGO blocks. According to Pine: What can you build with LEGO bricks? Anything you want, thanks to the large number of modules (different sizes, shapes, & colors) and the simple & elegant linkage system for snapping them together. Then you must work with each individual customer, creating a design experience through a tool that helps customers figure out what they want. To see great mass customization in action, refer to what NIKE is doing. Through its NIKEiD service, it gives customers a truly personalized footwear experience, allowing them to build their own pair from scratch. Customers can go online, select the type of shoe they want to design & customize its look, fit, & performance. Everything can be personalized, from the material, to the color of the famous NIKE swoosh. Once they're satisfied, shoppers can just hit the "add to cart" button and proceed to checkout.

Mechanic's Lien: Claim created by state statutes to secure priority of payment of the price & value of work performed & materials furnished in constructing, repairing or improving a building or other structure, & which attaches to the land as well as to the buildings and improvements thereon.

Medical Office Building (MOB): Structure with at least 75% of its interior built out to accommodate healthcare providers such as doctors & dentists or healthcare technicians who perform exams with specialized equipment. Usually, the buildings have more robust mechanical, electrical & plumbing systems & reinforced floors to accommodate numerous exam rooms & heavy medical equipment.

Metes and Bounds: The boundary lines of land, with their terminal points and angles, described by listing the compass directions and distances of the boundaries. Originally, metes referred to distance & bounds referred to direction.

Mezzanine Office: Office space that is built in an industrial facility. It is usually along the perimeter of a facility and creates an intermediate floor.

Mixed Use: Space within a building or project providing for more than one use (i.e., a loft or apartment project with retail, an apartment building with office space, and an office building with retail space).

Mixed Use Development: The grouping of multiple significant uses within a single site or building such as retail, office, residential or lodging facilities. Examples include office buildings that contain ground-level retail and housing, plus projects that have separate office, retail and multifamily properties. Clustering of at least three different uses such as office, retail, residential and/or hotel adjacent to or in close walkable proximity to one another. Uses can be contained in the same building or dispersed in different buildings that are adjacent to or close to one another.

197

Mobile Payments: Pertains to the services & technology that enable consumers to pay using their mobile phones, instead of traditional forms of payment like cash or credit cards. Mobile payment solutions come in many forms. The most popular ones include NFC-based solutions such as Apple Pay or Google Wallet, & app-based solutions like PayPal.

Mobile Shopping: Increasingly common trend thanks to the popularity of smartphones & tablets, mobile shopping is purchasing goods or services using a mobile device. Mobile shoppers can complete their transactions either on a retailer's mobile site or with the use of an app.

Modified Lease: Lease in which the landlord receives a stipulated rent, and payment of the property's operating expenses is divided between the lessor and lessee via specified terms in the lease. Also called "Modified Gross," "Net-net" (Double Net), "Net-net-net" (Triple Net), depending on the degree to which the tenant or landlord are responsible for operating costs.

Multitenant Office Building: A building that is not owner occupied and space that is leased to two or more tenants.

Mystery Shopping: This is an activity practiced by market research companies, watchdog groups, or even retailers themselves to evaluate product or service quality or compliance. The mystery shopper acts like a regular consumer and performs tasks like asking questions, submitting complaints, or simply completing a purchase like they normally would. They would then provide feedback or write reports detailing their experience with the retailer.

N

**Neighborhood
Shopping Center:** This type of retail property is most commonly found in the U.S. Anchored by supermarkets and drug stores, the centers are typically one-level, rectangular structures with surface parking in the front and merchandise loading areas in the back. They provide for the sale of convenience goods (food, drugs, etc.) & personal services (laundry, dry cleaning, etc.) for the day-to-day living needs of the immediate neighborhood.

Net Absorption: The net change in occupied space over a specified period of time. This change is measured in square feet at the building, submarket & market levels. This figure reflects the amount of space occupied as well as the amount of space vacated. Net absorption can be either positive or negative & must reflect increases & decreases in inventory levels.

Net Cashflow: Annual income produced by an investment property after deducting allowances for capital repairs, leasing commissions, tenant inducements (after the initial lease is up) & debt service from net operating income.

Net Lease: Lease in which there is a provision for the tenant to pay, in addition to rent, certain costs associated with the operation of the property. They may include property taxes, insurance, repairs, utilities, & maintenance. There are also "NN" (double net) & "NNN" (triple net) leases. The difference between the 3 is the degree to which the tenant is responsible for operating costs.

Net Operating Income (NOI): Income generated after deducting operating expenses but before deducting taxes and financing expenses.

Net Rentable Area: Floor area of a building that remains after the square footage represented by vertical penetrations, such as elevator shafts, has been deducted. Common areas & mechanical rooms are included & there are no deductions for necessary columns & projections of the building.

New Space: Space delivered to the market that was never previously leased or occupied by a tenant.

Niche Retailing: Refers to the practice of selling only to a specific market segment. A niche retailer specializes in a particular type of product (or sometimes a few closely related ones). They can be more nimble with their strategies, compared to broader businesses because they cater to specific audiences. This enables them to identify market segments easily & deploy unique & more targeted strategies to address their market's needs. A good example of a niche retailer is Sunglass Hut, a popular retail chain that specializes in selling sunglasses.

Non-Compete Clause: A clause that can be inserted into a lease specifying that the business of the tenant is exclusive in the property and that no other tenant operating the same or similar type of business can occupy space in the building. This clause benefits service-oriented businesses desiring exclusive access to the building's population (i.e. travel agent, deli, etc.).

Non-Disclosure Agreement (NDA): Legally enforceable contract that creates a confidential relationship between a person who holds a trade secret & a person to whom the secret will be disclosed. These agreements typically serve 3 key functions:

1. NDAs protect sensitive information. By signing it, participants promise to not divulge or release information shared with them by the other people involved. If leaked, the injured person can claim breach of contract.

2. In the case of new product or concept development, a confidentiality agreement can help the inventor keep patent rights. In many cases, public disclosure of a new invention can void patent rights. A properly drafted NDA can help the original creator hold onto the rights to a product or idea.

3. Confidentiality agreements & NDAs expressly outline what is private & what's fair game. In many cases, the agreement serves as a document that classifies exclusive & confidential information.

Normal Wear and Tear: The deterioration or loss in value caused by the tenant's normal and reasonable use. In many leases the tenant is not responsible for "normal wear and tear".

O

**Occupancy
Cost:** Includes rent, real estate & personal property taxes, plus insurance, depreciation & amortization expenses. The actual dollars paid out by the tenant to occupy the space. It can be expressed in either pre-tax or after tax dollars.

**Occupied
Space:** Space physically occupied by a tenant, subtenant or owner. It is calculated by subtracting total vacant space from total competitive inventory. If subtenant space is excluded from the calculation, then the term "direct occupied space" is recommended.

**Offering
Memorandum:** Legally binding document used to provide information relevant to the process of a financial transaction. Sometimes referred to as a prospectus, it may be required when offering stocks to investors, or selling real estate. In any situation, the document will include data that is required by law to be supplied to investors, ensuring they have sufficient information to make an informed decision about making the purchase.

Office Building: Structure providing environments that are conducive to the performance of management & administrative activities, accounting, marketing, information processing, consulting, human resources management, financial & insurance services, educational & medical services, & other professional services. At least 75% of the interior space is finished to accommodate office users, but the rest of the space can include other uses such as retail, restaurant or fitness.

Office Building Classifications: The real estate industry uses a subjective classification system that divides buildings into three qualitative categories: Class A, Class B & Class C. Building classifications are relative & applied to all buildings that make up the competitive inventory in a market. A building that is Class A in a second-tier market may not be Class A in a first-tier market. The designations are determined primarily on the basis of building locations or submarkets, rents, building systems & finishes, and building upkeep and services

**Office Building
Types and Sizes**: <u>Low-rise</u>: Fewer than 7 stories above ground level
<u>Mid-rise</u>: Between 7 and 25 stories above ground level
<u>High-rise</u>: More than 25 stories above ground level

Office Condo: Short for "office condominium," this term refers to the ownership structure of an office property in which individual units housed in one structure are sold to independent owners. Typically, there are covenants that govern the activities that can be carried out in and improvements that can be made to each unit. Such covenants also stipulate the distribution of costs related to the maintenance and operations of common elements in the building such as the roof and the elevators.

**Office Park
(Campus)**: Contiguous acres of land, master-planned with roads, sidewalks and trails, and extensive landscaping that accommodate stand-alone office buildings with adjacent surface parking lots or parking structures.

**Office
Percentage**: The percentage of total square feet in an industrial building that is built for use as office space. When the mezzanine office is built above a space that would otherwise be an industrial work area, this additional square footage is not counted in the total square footage of the building.

**Omni-Channel
Retailing**: The next generation of cross-channel & multi-channel retail. Omni-channel means establishing a presence on several channels & platforms (i.e. brick-and-mortar, mobile, online, etc.) & enabling customers to transact, interact, & engage across the channels simultaneously or interchangeably. Giving the customer the convenience & flexibility to purchase an item using an app, then letting them pick up the purchase in the store, plus allowing them to process a return via the website, is an example of omni-channel retailing. It goes beyond simply being on multiple channels or platforms. Just having a website, a mobile app, & a physical store doesn't necessarily mean that you're an omni-channel retailer. In order to truly be one, you must fuse all those channels together to give customers a seamless experience.

Online or Pure Play Retailer: Retailer that sells exclusively online & does not have any brick-and mortar retail locations.

Operating Cost Escalation: Clauses that adjust rents by reference to external standards such as published indexes, negotiated wage levels, or expenses related to the ownership & operation of buildings. Most landlords pass through proper & customary charges, but in the hands of an overly aggressive landlord, these clauses can operate to impose obligations which the tenant would not willingly or knowingly accept.

Operating Expenses: Actual costs associated with operating a property including maintenance, repairs, management, utilities, taxes & insurance. A landlord's definition of operating expenses is likely to be quite broad, covering most aspects of operating the building.

Operating Expense Escalation: Although there are many variations of operating expense escalation clauses, all are intended to adjust rents by reference to external standards such as published indexes, negotiated wage levels, or expenses related to the ownership & operation of buildings.

Opportunistic Investment: Ground-up development of a real estate project is considered an opportunistic investment. It is an investment in a parcel or site that typically involves some or all of the following: rezoning for use or density or both; net new or ground-up construction; conversion of a building from one use to another; complete gut or significant rehab of a building, requiring that it be entirely vacant to complete; introduction of uses not previously seen on this parcel or in this area; etc.

Owner Occupied Office Building: Buildings that are occupied by the owner & that generally are not included in the competitive inventory.

Outlet: Indicates a shopping center comprised primarily of factory outlet stores where manufacturers sell product at a discount. Outlet centers are often but not always open-air rather than enclosed shopping centers.

P

Parking Ratio or Index: The intent of this ratio is to provide a uniform method of expressing the amount of parking that is available at a given building. Dividing the total rentable square footage of a building by the building's total number of parking spaces provides the amount of rentable square feet per each individual parking space (expressed as 1/xxx or 1 per xxx). Dividing 1000 by the previous result provides the ratio of parking spaces available per each 1000 rentable square feet (expressed as x per 1000).

Partial Taking: The taking of part (a portion) of an owner's property under the laws of eminent domain.

Pass Through: Also called C.A.M., this refers to the tenant's Pro rata: Proportionately; according to measure, interest, or liability. In the case of a tenant, the proportionate share of expenses for the maintenance & operation of the property and of operating expenses (i.e. taxes, utilities, repairs) paid in addition to the base rent.

Percentage Lease: Refers to a provision of the lease calling for the landlord to be paid a percentage of the tenant's gross sales as a component of rent. There is usually a base rent amount to which "percentage" rent is then added. This type of clause is most often found in retail leases.

Performance Bond: A surety bond posted by a contractor guaranteeing full performance of a contract with the proceeds to be used to complete the contract or compensate for the owner's loss in the event of nonperformance.

Planogram: This is a visual representation that shows how merchandise should be arranged on store shelves in order to drive more sales. It's a model that indicates the best placement and positioning of your merchandise. Remember that product positioning can influence consumers' purchases, so planning how they're displayed and organized can maximize sales. Planograms can also guide and assist in store mapping and they enable retailers use space more effectively.

Point of Sale
(POS) System: At its most basic level, a POS system functions as a cash register or till system that lets retailers ring up sales and keep a record of those transactions in their stores. But thanks to advancements in technology, POS systems - or ePOS systems - can now extend beyond the point of sale. These days, many POS solutions serve as retail management systems that handle everything from sales and inventory, to customer management and ecommerce.

Pop-Up Store: Pop-up-stores are short-term shops or sales spaces that come and go within a given period. These stores can be set up in empty retail spaces, mall booths, or even in the middle of a park. A retail store, restaurant or kiosk intentionally designed to be in a location for a finite amount of time (i.e., a restaurant that opens for six months so it can test a market, or a store that operates in a location during the holiday season only).

Power Center: Indicates a shopping center that generally contains three or more category-dominant anchors, including discount department stores, off-price stores, wholesale clubs, and relatively few small tenants. Among the largest types of retail properties, they typically feature three or more big box retailers such as Home Depot, Target and Walmart. Various smaller retailers are usually clustered together in a community shopping center configuration. Power centers are typically made up of multiple large buildings that are one-level, rectangular structures with surface parking in the front and merchandise loading areas in the back. Often, more money is spent on features and architecture at these locations than at big box shopping centers.

Pre-leased: Refers to space in a proposed building that has been leased before the start of construction or in advance of the issuance of a Certificate of Occupancy. The term applies to space that has been leased in a building that is under construction.

Prestige Pricing: Usually implemented by high-end retailers & lifestyle brands, prestige pricing is a strategy in which an item is priced at a high level in order to denote exclusivity, high quality, or luxury. When an item is prestigiously priced, it is meant to attract status-conscious individuals or consumers who want to buy premium products. Louis Vuitton is a prime example of a retailer with a prestige pricing strategy. The French fashion house has premium pricing on all its products, doesn't conduct sales or have outlet stores.

Prime Tenant: The major or anchor tenant in a building or shopping center serving to attract other, smaller tenants into adjacent space because of the customer traffic generated.

Private Label: Brands owned not by a manufacturer, but by a retailer or supplier. Retailers & suppliers purchase the goods, then label & market them under their name.

Pro rata: Proportionately; according to measure, interest or liability. In the case of a tenant, the proportionate share of expenses for the maintenance & operation of the property.

Pro Rata Share: The percentage that, when multiplied by reimbursable expenses (less an expense stop if referring to a gross lease), equals the amount to be reimbursed by a tenant to the landlord for expense recoveries. Typically, the percentage is calculated by dividing the net rentable area of a tenant's leased premises by the net rentable area of the building, although this isn't always the case.

Proposed or Planned: A building that has received zoning approval but has not yet started construction.

Punch List: Itemized list, typically prepared by the architect or construction manager, documenting incomplete or unsatisfactory items after the contractor has notified the owner that the tenant space is substantially complete.

Push-back Rack: In industrial uses a racking system with a sliding device that pushes back pallets, allowing multiple pallets to be placed in the same location.

Q

Quack: A pretender, charlatan, imposter…you see these in both public and private sector people. Elected officials as well. These people hinder development and cost both sides time and money.

Quality of Life: Hard to define, but when a community has it, everybody knows it. Retail development, when it's done the right way, always raises the bar on quality of life in a city.

Quit Claim Deed: A quit claim deed is a legal instrument which is used to transfer interest in real property. The entity transferring its interest is called the grantor, and when the quitclaim deed is properly completed and executed it transfers any interest the grantor has in the property to a recipient, called the grantee.

R

Radio Frequency Identification (RFID): Inventory tracking technology embedded in devices that are attached to labels on packages so an item's location can be tracked.

Rail Door: A door that is generally side-loading, that has access to railroad tracks, and facilitates the loading or unloading of goods from a railroad car to an industrial building.

Rail Service: A railroad spur adjacent to a building structure that allows the building to be served by rail operations.

Ramp Door: A dock-high door that has been converted to a drive-in door by creating a ramp from ground level to dock level.

Real Estate Investment Trust (REIT): A company that owns or finances income-producing assets, such as apartments, shopping centers, offices & warehouses. It may also invest in air or water rights, un-harvested crops, permanent structures & structural components that are part of a structure but don't themselves produce income. Shares of REITs can be traded like stocks & can allow owners of the shares to participate in the real estate market.

Real Estate Owned (REO): Sale in which a lender, either institutional or private, sells a property that the lender has taken back through foreclosure.

Real Property: Land, and generally whatever is erected or affixed to the land, such as buildings, fences, and including light fixtures, plumbing and heating fixtures, or other items which would be personal property if not attached.

Recapitalization: When owners liquidate some or most of their ownership position in an asset by selling some or most of their equity position.

Recapture: Clause giving the lessor a percentage of profits above a fixed amount of rent; or in a percentage lease, a clause granting the landlord a right to terminate the lease if the tenant fails to realize minimum sales.

Redevelopment: Building or site that involves teardown & rebuilding of most-if not all- structures on that site. This change typically occurs in sought-after areas that are usually well located, where buildings have become unattractive, obsolete or where there is a demand for different uses.

Regional Shopping Center: Among the largest types of retail properties, it typically features large anchor tenants that sell general merchandise & fashion. Historically configured like traditional suburban malls, many have evolved to town center or main street retail formats. Parking is accommodated via surface or structure spaces or both.

Relationship Retailing: A strategy businesses implement to build loyalty & forge long-term relationships with customers. Relationship retailing can come in the form of loyalty programs, personalized experiences, or superb customer service.

Re-let Space: Sometimes called "second-generation space," it refers to existing space that was previously occupied by a tenant.

Renewal Option: Also called, option to renew, this is a clause giving a tenant the right to extend the term of a lease, usually for a stated period of time and at a rent amount as provided for in the option language. The right of a tenant to extend the lease term for a specified period of time at a predefined rental rate. In many instances, the rate is defined as a percentage of market rent, and in other instances, the rate is a specified dollar amount. An auto-renewal option is where the lease term is extended automatically on the expiration date without any notification requirement. Often, there is a date by which this option must be executed; otherwise, the option expires.

221

Renovation: Upgrading & modernizing common areas in a building such as lobbies, bathrooms, parking areas, etc. The tenant remains in the building, & the building use & square footage don't change. It's often done together with a retrofit.

Rent: Compensation or fee paid, usually periodically (monthly payments, for occupancy & use of rental property, land, buildings, equipment, etc.).

Rent Commencement Date: Date a tenant begins paying rent. The dynamics of the marketplace will dictate if the date coincides with the definition or if it commences months later (in a weak market the tenant may be granted several months free rent). It will never begin before the lease commencement date.

Rentable Building Area (RBA): Total square footage of a building that can be occupied by or assigned to a tenant for the purpose of determining a tenant's total rental obligation. Generally, it includes common areas including hallways, lobbies, bathrooms & phone/ data closets.

222

Rentable Square Footage: Rentable square footage equals the usable square footage plus the tenant's pro rata share of the building common areas, such as lobbies, public corridors & restrooms. The pro-rata share, often referred to as the rentable/usable (R/U) factor, will typically be at least 1.10 and may be higher for more inefficient buildings (such as historic rehabilitations) or for partial floors.

Rentable / Usable Ratio (R/U): Number obtained when the total rentable area in a building is divided by the usable area. The inverse of this ratio describes the proportion of space that an occupant can expect to actually utilize or physically occupy.

Rental Concession: Also called rent abatement or free rent, this is a concession a landlord may offer a tenant in order to secure their tenancy. While it is one form of a concession, there are many others such as increased tenant improvement allowance, signage, lower than market rental rates & moving allowances are only a few of the many.

Rent-Up Period: Period of time following construction of a new building, when tenants are actively being sought & the project is approaching its stabilized occupancy.

Representation Agreement: Agreement between the owner of a property and a real estate broker giving the broker the authorization to attempt to sell or lease the property at a certain price and terms in return for a commission, set fee or other form of compensation.

Restaurant: Place where people pay to sit & eat meals that are cooked & served on the premises.

Retail Flagship: Flagship stores serve as retailers' main stores & are aimed at serving large numbers of customers. They are found in prominent shopping districts & target high-income shoppers. They are typically larger than outlet or mall stores & hold large volumes of merchandise. A retailer's primary location, a store in a prominent location, a chain's largest store, the store that holds or sells the highest volume of merchandise, or a retailer's best known location.

Return on Investment (ROI): A measure of the value created by a real estate investment. It is the difference between the net gains from investing in the property less the net cost from investing in the property divided by the purchase price of the property. Usually, it is reported as a percentage.

Retrofit: Modernization of building systems such as heating, ventilation & air conditioning (HVAC), security, fire alarms & energy management. The tenant remains in the building, & the building use & square footage do not change. It is often done together with a renovation.

Right of First Refusal: A lease clause giving a tenant the first opportunity to buy or lease a property at the same price and on the same terms and conditions as those contained in a third party offer that the owner has expressed a willingness to accept. Such rights often pertain to adjacent space.

S

Sale-Leaseback: Essentially a financing transaction where the owner occupant of a property agrees to sell all or part of the property to an investor and then lease it back and continue to occupy space as a tenant. Although the lease technically follows the sale, both will have been agreed to as part of the same transaction. An owner-occupied property that is sold to a third-party investor. The previous owner becomes the tenant that pays rent to the new owner. This tactic allows property owners to convert their ownership (equity) into cash while still occupying the property. The seller's (now the tenant's) lease term must be for two or more years.

Security Deposit: A deposit of money by a tenant to a landlord to secure performance of a lease. This deposit can also take the form of a letter of credit or other financial instrument.

Secured Compartmental Information Facility: Highly secure space that meets specialized design guidelines and restrictions for building systems relating to data, power, communications, security, ductwork, ventilation and more. The highly controlled facilities are required by firms such as defense contractors or law firms that deal in sensitive industries.

Self-Serve: In retail, this means letting customers select and pay for goods themselves, without requiring the assistance of a live staff member. Vending machines, kiosks, as well as self-serve checkout lanes in grocery stores all fall under this category.

Service Center or Showroom: A type of flex facility characterized by a substantial showroom area, usually fronting a freeway or major road.

Shadow Space: A portion of leased space that is not being used by the tenant. This area can include unused space that a tenant leased and is holding for expected future growth. It can also include unused space that was previously occupied but is no longer used as a result of downsizing the company's workforce. Shadow space is difficult to measure because it isn't officially marketed or tracked in industry databases.

Shell Space: Space within a property that is currently not built out.

Short Sale: When the sale price of an asset is less than the amount owed to the lender and when the lender accepts this amount as full payment for the loan. Those funds not repaid to the lender will be written off.

Shrinkage: The difference between the amounts of stock on paper and the actual stock available. In other words, it's a reduction in inventory that isn't caused by legit sales. The common causes of shrinkage include employee theft, shoplifting, administrative errors, and supplier fraud.

Showrooming: Showrooming is the consumer practice of examining products in a store, only to buy them for a lower price online. Shopping and price check apps perpetuate showrooming because they allow shoppers to compare prices and products using their phone as they browse the store.

Side-loading Dock: In industrial settings a loading dock configuration designed to facilitate the loading and unloading of a vehicle through its side.

Single-tenant Office Building: A building for which there is a single lease obligation.

Slab: The exposed wearing surface laid over the structural support beams of a building to form the floor(s) of the building or laid slab-on-grade in the case of a non-structural, ground level concrete slab.

Social Commerce: S-Commerce refers to retail models or ecommerce practices that incorporate social media, user-generated content or social interaction. The role of social sites like Facebook or Twitter in S-Commerce isn't necessarily to serve as platforms for buying & selling; rather, they're meant to assist the process & help drive sales. According to Mashable, the 7 species of social commerce are:

1. Peer-to-peer sales platforms (eBay, Etsy, Amazon Marketplace)
2. Social network-driven sales (Facebook, Pinterest, Twitter)
3. Group buying (Groupon, LivingSocial)
4. Peer recommendations (Amazon, Yelp, JustBoughtIt)
5. User-curated shopping (The Fancy, Lyst, Svpply)
6. Participatory commerce (Threadless, Kickstarter, CutOnYourBias)
7. Social shopping (Motilo, Fashism, GoTryItOn)

Threadless is an online apparel store that sources its designs from its community. It enables artists to earn money & recognition for their designs by allowing them to submit their creations to the site. The social commerce aspect kicks in when the community votes & scores the submissions to determine which designs are chosen for print. The winning artists are then paid with cash prizes as well as royalties from their shirt sales.

Space Plan: A graphic representation of a tenant's space requirements, showing wall & door locations, room sizes, & sometimes includes furniture layouts. A preliminary space plan will be prepared for a prospective tenant at any number of different properties & this serves as a "test-fit" to help the tenant determine which property will best meet its requirements. When the tenant has selected a building of choice, a final space plan is prepared which speaks to all of the landlord & tenant objectives & then approved by both parties. It must be sufficiently detailed to allow an accurate estimate of the construction costs. This final space plan will often become an exhibit to any lease negotiated between the parties.

Special Assessment: Any special charge levied against real property for public improvements (sidewalks, streets, water & sewer) that benefit the assessed property.

Speculative Space: Any tenant space that has not been leased before the start of construction on a new building. A building developed & constructed without any preleasing in place. Construction commences without a prelease when the developer believes there is so much demand for that type of building in that market or submarket that a lease commitment is bound to come through.

Stabilized Cap Rate: The ratio between the net operating income produced by a property upon achieving target occupancy, & its purchase value.

Stacking Plan: A floor-by-floor & suite-by-suite graphical representation within a building. The plan shows the suite number, the square footage & the tenant occupying each suite. On many stacking plans, lease expiration dates are also provided to give a quick view of the occupancy exposure within a building.

Step-Up Lease (Graded Lease): A lease specifying set increases in rent at set intervals during the term of the lease.

Straight Lease (Flat Lease): A lease specifying the same, a fixed amount, of rent that is to be paid periodically during the entire term of the lease. This is typically paid out in monthly installments.

Straight Line Rent: The accumulation of rental income (including months that have free rent, discounted rent & fixed-rent increases) divided by the term of the lease will generate a straight-line rent. Straight-line rent provides a way to compare rents on various properties using a consistent methodology.

Strip Shopping Center: An attached row of stores or service outlets that are managed as a coherent retail entity with onsite parking usually located in front of the stores. Open canopies may connect the storefronts, but a strip center does not have enclosed walkways linking the stores. It may be configured in a straight line or may have an "L" or "U" shape.

Stock Keeping Unit: More commonly known as SKU, it pertains to the unique identification of a particular product. It's used in inventory management & enables retailers to track & distinguish. It represents all the attributes of an item, including style, brand, size, color etc.

Strip Center / Retail Park: Shopping center that is not enclosed & its stores' entrances typically face the parking lot.

Sublet Space: Space offered for lease indirectly by a tenant rather than directly by a landlord.

Submarket: Geographic divisions of markets. These smaller divisions or boundaries are generally recognized & accepted by the real estate industry & the business community in a market & region. They are geographic boundaries that delineate core areas that are competitive with one another, & together they constitute a generally accepted secondary set of competitive areas. In the real estate industry, submarkets are building-type specific & are non-overlapping contiguous geographic designations with a cumulative sum that matches the boundaries of a market. They contain properties sufficient to provide information for aggregate statistics.

Suburban: Suburban means a geographic area that contains a variety of property types arranged in a setting that is less dense than neighboring urban areas. This broad term can be defined or measured a number of ways and is often defined relative to urban and exurban areas.

Subordination Agreement: As used in a lease, the tenant generally accepts the leased premises subject to any recorded mortgage or deed of trust lien and all existing recorded restrictions, and the landlord is often given the power to subordinate the tenant's interest to any first mortgage or deed of trust lien subsequently placed upon the leased premises.

Super Flat Floors: Concrete floors with minimal variations in elevation from point to point. The floors are found primarily in warehouses with automated systems. Precisely calibrated & leveled picking machinery & racks require level flooring to ensure proper operation.

Super-regional Shopping Center: The enclosed, large anchor tenants that sell general merchandise and fashion offer more variety than does a regional center.

Sustainable Development: In commercial real estate (CRE), this term means the practice of developing, redeveloping & operating CRE in ways that cause zero, minimal or improved environmental impact.

T

Taking: Synonym for condemnation or any actual or material interference with private property rights but it is not essential that there be physical seizure or appropriation.

Takeup: When the space is physically occupied.

Tenant (Lessee): One who rents real estate from another and holds an estate by virtue of a lease.

Tenants or Tenancy in Common (TIC): An estate held by two or more persons, each of whom has an undivided interest, which means that each party has the right to sell or transfer the ownership of his or her ownership interest.

Tenant at Will: One who holds possession of premises by permission of the owner or landlord, the characteristics of which are an uncertain duration (i.e. without a fixed term) and the right of either party to terminate on proper notice.

**Tenant
Improvements:** Improvements made to the leased premises by or for a tenant. Generally, especially in new space, part of the negotiations will include in some detail the improvements to be made in the leased premises by the landlord.

**Tenant
Improvements
Allowance:** Allowance or Work Letter: Defines the fixed amount of money contributed by the landlord toward tenant improvements. The tenant pays any of the costs that exceed this amount. Also commonly referred to as "Tenant Finish Allowance".

Theatre: A building, part of a building, or outdoor area for housing dramatic presentations, stage entertainments, or motion-picture shows.

**Third Party
Logistics
(3PL):** Businesses that provide one or more logistics services including multi-client warehousing, contract warehousing, transportation management, distribution management, inventory management & freight consolidation.

**Time Is Of
The Essence**: The performance by one party within the period specified in the contract is essential to require performance by the other party.

**Total
Inventory**: Total number of buildings & total square footage (net rentable area) in the competitive inventory. Buildings under construction are not part of included. Total inventory increases when a new building is delivered & decreases when an existing building is demolished or changes use. It includes properties under renovation if the building remains inhabitable during the process but excludes properties converting to a different use. It is typically measured at the submarket & market levels. A description of the characteristics & numeric thresholds that make up the total inventory should be provided. The figure may vary from one data provider to another as a result of tailored definitions of what constitutes the competitive inventory.

**Town
Center**: Historical term used to refer to the commercial, civic or geographic center of a community. Today, the term is associated with retail & has come to be known as a robust retail cluster with civic or open spaces in proximity to a variety of uses such as residential, office, retail & hotel.

Trade Fixtures: Personal property that is attached to a structure (i.e. the walls of the leased premises) that are used in the business. Since this property is part of the business and not deemed to be part of the real estate, it is typically removable upon lease termination.

Traditional Outlet: The tenants offer a discount version of mainstream retailers and are often called "factory stores." They usually focus on apparel. Traditionally, the stores have been located far outside a city center. The outlets are designed as a destination or tourist magnet.

Traditional Retailer: A retailer that started selling in brick-and-mortar locations but that now also sells items online.

Transit-Oriented Development (TOD): Real estate projects that are built around transit to maximize access to shared transportation modes. Typically, the TOD project is dense & walkable, & it includes a mix of uses such as residential, office, retail, hotel & entertainment.

Transit Score: A number between 0 and 100 that measures the relative usefulness of nearby routes. "Usefulness" is typically measured by a weighted algorithm of characteristics such as distance to the nearest stop; mode of the route such as bus, ferry or rail & frequency of service.

90–100 Rider's Paradise World-class public transportation
70–89 Excellent Transit convenient for most trips
50–69 Good Transit Many nearby public transportation options
25–49 Some Transit A few nearby public transportation options
0–24 Minimal Transit Possible to get on a bus

Tribetailing: This term refers to the retail practice of tailoring everything you do–from your store design, to your ads, to your employees–for a specific tribe or group of people. With Tribetailing, you're not trying to please the public or the masses. Instead, you're zeroing in on a particular niche and are catering to them and only them.

Triple Net Rent (NNN): Lease in which the tenant pays, in addition to rent, certain costs associated with a property, which may include property taxes, insurance premiums, repairs, utilities & maintenances. There are also "Net Leases" & "NN" (double net) leases, depending upon the degree to which the tenant is responsible for operating costs. A lease agreement whereby the tenant pays taxes, maintenance & property insurance as well as all operating costs associated with the tenant's occupancy, including personal property taxes, janitorial services & all utility costs. The landlord is responsible for the roof & structure & sometimes the parking lot.

Trophy Building: Landmark property located in a highly desirable submarket designed by a recognized architect, & features high-end finishes & modern or efficient systems. It commands among the highest rents & is more than 80% occupied by the market's premier tenants. It is highly sought after by institutional investors such as pension funds & insurance companies & foreign investors. They are more desirable than Class A buildings.

Truck Court: Exterior area adjacent to an industrial building's loading docks where trucks maneuver. The most important measure of the truck court is the depth from the building to the end of the truck court. Greater depth allows for greater maneuverability and better accommodates multiple trucks.

Truck Terminal: This specialized distribution building for redistributing goods from one truck to another serves as an intermediate transfer point. The facilities are primarily used for staging loads (rather than long-term storage) & possess very little, if any, storage area.

Truck Turning Radius: The tightest turn a truck can make, depending on several variables such as truck configuration, trailer size and location of adjacent objects that obstruct the inner turning radius.

Truss: A framework of beams forming a rigid structure (as in a roof truss).

Truss Height: Distance from the floor to the bottom edge of a truss used to support the ceiling or roof of a building. If there are hanging objects, beams or joists below the truss, the clear height will be lower than the truss height.

**Turn Key Project
or Premises**: The construction of a project in which a third party, usually a developer or general contractor, is responsible for the total completion of a building (including construction & interior design) or, the construction of tenant improvements to the customized requirements & specifications of a future owner or tenant. Refers to the fact that the space is completely constructed & ready for occupancy, & the tenant need only "turn the key" to occupy the space (i.e., no further work is necessary). A term used to describe a landlord's agreement to provide and pay for improvements to a tenant's premises. The landlord is required to deliver the premises in a condition ready for the tenant's stipulated use.

U

Unanchored: Indicates that the center has no anchor tenant or major retailer in place.

Under Construction: A building is under construction when construction permits have been obtained & site excavation has begun. If a site is being redeveloped, demolition of existing structures doesn't necessarily indicate that construction has begun. Sites are sometimes cleared years in advance of a groundbreaking.

Under Renovation: A building is under renovation when construction permits have been obtained & demolition has begun. It's under renovation if it remains inhabitable by tenants during the construction. If an existing building is gutted extensively (i.e., elevators & bathrooms don't function & it can't be occupied by a tenant), then the building should be removed from inventory & redelivered when the occupancy permit is issued.

**Unified Brand
Experience:** In retail, this concept is all about establishing a consistent brand or identity throughout multiple channels or platforms, including brick-and-mortar, ecommerce, or mobile. So whether you're marketing and selling to customers face-to-face, on your mobile app, or doing it online, you'll be able to deliver the same messages and give them the same great experience. Successfully implementing this involves properly training your staff, investing in the right tools, and more importantly, having one clear strategy and message.

Urban: Urban areas are commonly identified with a city, are typically built on a traditional street grid, have consistent building setbacks, have sidewalks and usually include multiple-story building

Use: The specific purpose for which a parcel of land or a building is intended to be used as specified in the lease's use clause.

Usable Area: This relative term is best compared to rentable area. Usable area is the amount of space that can actually be used by tenants within the space they lease. For example, columns inside a tenant space are counted in the measure of rentable area, but the space occupied by the column cannot be used by the tenant. A tenant's usable area does not include common areas in the building.

Usable Square Footage: Usable square footage is the area contained within the demising walls of the tenant space. Total usable square footage equals the net square footage x the circulation factor. Also see circulation factor and net square footage.

V

Vacancy Factor: The amount of gross revenue that pro forma income statements anticipate will be lost because of vacancies, often expressed as a percentage of the total rentable square footage available in a building or project.

Vacancy Rate: The total amount of available space compared to the total inventory of space and expressed as a percentage. This is calculated by multiplying the vacant space times 100 and then dividing it by the total inventory. A measurement expressed as a percentage of the total amount of vacant space divided by the total amount of inventory. This measurement is typically applied to a building, a submarket or a market.

Vacant Space: Inventory that is not currently occupied. If subtenant space is excluded from the calculation, the term "direct vacant space" is recommended.

Value Add Investment: An investment in a real estate asset with existing cash flow (and value) that can be increased by raising occupancy, rents or both. Owners typically carry out one or more of the following to add value to a building: improve or replace building systems, provide new finishes, introduce new amenities, improve access or circulation to the building, add square footage, etc.

W

Walk Score: Number between 0 and 100 that measures amenities such as retail, businesses, parks, theaters & schools that can be accessed by foot inside a 1-mile radius from a particular address.

90–100 Walker's Paradise daily errands do not require a car
70–89 Very walkable most errands can be accomplished on foot
50–69 Some-what walkable some errands can be accomplished on foot
25–49 Car-dependent most errands require a car
0–24 Car-dependent almost all errands require a car

Warehouse: Facility primarily used for the storage or distribution or both of materials, goods & merchandise.

Web-rooming: Looking at products online before buying them in brick-and-mortar stores. The opposite of web-rooming, when customers look at products in stores & buy online. Image-based sites Pinterest & Instagram help perpetuate web-rooming. Users see items on the sites & go out to test or try them on.

Wearable Technology: Smartwatches, smartglasses, and fitness devices like FitBit all fall under the wearable tech. These are gadgets that people can wear, and they can often sync to an app or other cloud-based software. Wearable technology can have some interesting applications in retail. For instance, merchants can potentially use them to gain insights into customer movement, activity, and behavior as they move about the real world. On the backend, wearable tech can allow retail employees to do tasks such inventory counts hands-free. It can also aid communication by enabling team members to communicate with each other without having to use hand-held devices.

Working Drawings: The set of plans for a building or project that comprise the contract documents that indicate the precise manner in which a project is to be built. This set of plans includes a set of specifications for the building or project.

Work Letter: A list of the building standard items that the landlord will contribute as part of the tenant improvements as an incentive to lease property. Examples of the building standard items typically identified include style and type of doors, lineal feet of partitions, type and quantity of lights, quality of floor coverings, number of telephone and electrical outlets, etc. The work letter often carries a dollar value but is contrasted with a fixed dollar tenant improvement allowance that can be used at the tenant's discretion. A legal document that outlines the obligations of the landlord relative to the improvements necessary to prepare leased premises for a tenant's occupancy. Items typically found in a work letter include a description of the improvements, the cost thereof, and the portion of the cost to be paid by the landlord, the completion date and the insurance requirements of contractors performing the improvements.

Y

Year Built: The year the building was delivered to the market as a result of completed construction.

Year Renovated: The year the building last received a certificate of occupancy (COO) for a major renovation.

*[Special thanks to Adam Chandler, Tim Reddock, and NAIOP (National Association of Industrial and Office Properties), the Commercial Real Estate Development Association, is the leading organization for developers, owners, and related professionals in office, industrial, retail, and mixed use real estate.
NAIOP comprises some 18,000 members in North America. NAIOP advances responsible commercial real estate development and advocates for effective public policy. For more info, visit naiop.com

The Devil's in the Details

ACKNOWLEDGEMENTS

To all the fine people who have at one time or the other worked, assisted, gave advice, answered the phone, paid the bills, did the accounting, the marketing, kept the computers and servers working, kept the IRS happy, and flew the airplanes at Retail Attractions, LLC:

Wendy Hayes, Micah Hayes, Lauren Hayes, Joe Hayes, Beth and Rob Nichols, Randall Hayes, Josh Allen, Dawn McLarren, Courtney Dean Moseley, Sara Stephens, Tim Reddock, Adam Chandler, Marlo Thompson, Casey Reed, Kate Thorp, Mandy Vavrinak, Stephanie Moore, Caroline Winfrey, Bobby Busenberg, Zac Willis, Tom Swanson, Jessica Victoria Hunt, Tera Pogue, Pat Fry, Jeff Conklin, Ted Turner, Liz Pruitt, Julie Mullinex-Villanella, Dan Willard and a few more ☺.

To all our client cities, to their administrators, their elected officials, and the people who do the work. Thank you for all you do to assist us.

To the people I call for advice: Tom Kimball, Jim Shindler, Stephen Coslik, Jim Tapp, Roy and Jean Brashears, Jerry Reed, Rodney Ray, Brad Blakemore, Jim McGuire, Mike Mantle, Bob Parker, and others. Your assistance is deeply appreciated.

For help and editing and all around support on this book project: Stephanie Moore, Josh Allen, Adam Chandler, and Tim Reddock. Stephanie did a tremendous amount of work and was the go to girl on every issue, and Tim and Adam compiled a lot of the terms and definitions.

Special thanks to the two guys who challenged me to write: Page Cole and Sean Kouplen.

And finally, to a world class group of retail people, brokers, developers, attorneys, elected officials, city councilors, city planners, city managers, and others who have taught me, pushed me, made deals happen, and changed many cities for the better. Thanks to Dan Sullivan and Laura Townsend and all the people at the Grand River Dam Authority for allowing us to assist their customer communities, and to Tammye Gwin and Julie Mitchell and all the team at Choctaw Nations Business for allowing us to assist them in their economic development efforts and for all they do for the cities in their tribal boundaries.

To everybody else: those I forgot to mention, to all the good folks (you know who you are) and to all the ones who were not so good that taught me to choose my friends wisely, you all have been part of the tapestry of my life. I'm thankful and grateful for everything you contributed.

ABOUT THE COMPANY:

Retail Attractions, LLC was founded by Owner/CEO Rickey Hayes in 2007 to provide a suite of services to cities and other governmental entities who desire to see new retail development in their community and the increased sales tax and ad valorem tax revenue that retail and other commercial development brings to the community. Both communities and their citizens benefit when national retailers and restaurants, quality residential developments, state of the art health care and office facilities choose to locate in their city.

Our goal is to assist those responsible for bringing retail and other commercial development to cities and to make their jobs easier and more effective. Developers and retailers benefit from choosing a location in a Retail Attractions client city because our efforts are geared at helping the local governments make the development process smooth and efficient.

Potential sites are identified and pre-screened for any potential issues and quality, up-to-date market data is made available and kept current.

Our firm serves as a problem solving, solution-creating liaison between the public and the private sectors, which alleviates potential road blocks and helps make economic development successful. No matter how aggressively a retailer or restaurant desires to open a new unit in a specific location, there is always a real estate transaction involved. Pretty reports and all the data in the world will not make a real estate deal successful if the price of the dirt is out of alignment with market rates, or topographic issues, storm water issues, other utility and development issues, greed or any of a host of other issues arises.

Unlike our competitors, Retail Attractions began with the idea that the foundation of our services for our client communities should not solely consist of data, pretty presentations or reports. Our acute focus is grassroots, high-energy retail recruiting and market validation. The source of our continued success and effective retail recruitment is based on our relationships with the players in this field.

Our staff is focused on constant communication with established development groups and retail/restaurant connections, which ensures our client communities stay on the radar of growth driven tenants across a wide spectrum of the traditional retail and specialty outlet industry. We not only maintain these relationships, but our strategic focus on our client cities allows us to anticipate retail trends in the market and be one step ahead of our competitors.

One hundred percent of our client cities, that have worked with Retail Attractions and have made the effort to stay the course, have been patient with the process, have remained firmly engaged, have seen new retail development come to fruition in their city. Every single one of those cities has observed new private sector investment in their community. Our firm offers more to your community than mere data or demographics and goes far beyond flashy reports and maps. We believe effective retail recruitment accomplishes more than identifying which retailers might "fit" well within your city.

It takes more than strategies and more than coaching. It's about visualizing the reality of the community's retail potential, identifying the missing links in the local retail inventory, assessing the local real estate, and establishing a connection with the developer. Retail Attractions thrives directly in the role of the market validator, in closing the gap between the public and the private sector and connecting the retail and restaurant brands with the local real estate opportunities. Effective economic development is about relationships. Retail Attractions has them at every level of the retail spectrum and we put them to work for our clients, plain and simple.

While serving as the Economic Development Director for the City of Owasso for seven years, Rickey Hayes facilitated new commercial construction totaling more than 10 million square feet of retail and other mixed-use development. This construction produced more than half a billion dollars in total value, resulting in a city sales tax base more than triple what it had been before the new development.

Since beginning Retail Attractions, Rickey has helped cities launch millions of square feet of additional retail space and reap the associated benefits in additional revenues, goods and services for their citizens. As CEO of Retail Attractions, Rickey is a consultant not only to the private sector, but to cities, counties, economic development agencies, states and a couple of sovereign nations. Rickey and his team have worked in over 440 communities in 39 states, directly or indirectly in the eleven years they have been in the business of making communities better. Rickey has developed and extensive personal network of relationships in the areas of government relations, retail, restaurant and land development, real estate and site selection, leasing and tenanting and engineering. Rickey has also demonstrated success in producing effective, creative financing opportunities and incentives to expedite the success of public and private partnerships for development projects. Direct contact entails being contracted by a City, Chamber or EDC to recruit retail, restaurant, office and mixed-use development in a community, including medical, residential and multi-family development. Indirect contact indicates that a retailer, restaurant, developer or development company has contracted with us to offer them some form of developmental assistance, such as entitlements, annexation, zoning, incentives or other necessary consulting roles. We have effectively assisted cities in marketing their retail potential to national retailers and restaurants in every conceivable manner. Our scope of work includes local, regional and national efforts to make direct contact with not only real estate departments for retailers and restaurants, but also the corporate real estate contacts for these companies, as well as their tenant representatives, franchise owners, brokers, engineering firms and developers.

Retail Attractions, LLC can help your community reach its short and long term development and development related goals, identifying strategies to solve development problems, recruiting retail and restaurant tenants to your local lineup of existing retail providers, keeping your city's market data updated and available for local use and to provide your market data to the global spectrum of developers and retailers. Other services related to economic and retail development are available including marketing services for private and publicly owned real estate, aerial and drone photography, website development, social media services, public opinion surveys, citizen polls, economic impact studies, strategic and infrastructure planning and training public sector stakeholders on development issues.

RETAIL ATTRACTIONS, LLC STAFF INFORMATION:

Rickey Hayes: President and CEO

Micah Hayes: Data, Research, Mapping For Client Communities

Sara Stephens: Admin Assistant, Office Manager, Accounting, Retail Contacts

Rob Nichols: Web Site, Information Technology, Data Storage and Security

Beth Nichols: Deliverables, Marketing, Graphic Arts, Web Site Design

Stephanie Moore: Publications, Editing Services, Marketing, Public Opinion Surveys, Citizen Polls, Economic Impact Studies

Wendy Hayes: Retail Contacts, and Monthly Reporting

Ted Turner: Sales Tax Consultant

Ronald Cates: General Counsel- Legal

Josh Allen: Social Media / Marketing

CONTACT INFORMATION:

Retail Attractions, LLC
12150 East 96th Street North
Suite 107
Owasso, Oklahoma 74055

Phone: (918) 376-6707
Rickey Hayes cell: (918) 629-6066
Email: rickey@retailattractions.com
Email: office@retailattractions.com

ALSO WRITTEN BY RICKEY HAYES-

Available on Amazon.com or directly from
Retail Attractions, LLC by email at
office@retailattractions.com
or by phone at 918-386-6707

ENDORSEMENT FOR CITY ON A HILL A BOOK ON CITIES AND HOW TO MAKE THEM BETTER.

I first met Rickey Hayes several years ago in my capacity as a City Manager when we were introduced by our local Chamber of Commerce Director. She had worked with Mr. Hayes in the past and, based on their previous successes, believed that he could assist our city in capturing additional sales tax. While I was somewhat skeptical, I felt an obligation to at least hear him out, as I was the City Manager of a community, like so many others, that lives and dies by the amount of sales tax generated by the spending habits of our citizenry.

As Mr. Hayes made his presentation, complete with hard data and PowerPoint slides specific to our community, I became intrigued as I learned of the sales tax "leakage" our own residents were spending in surrounding communities and what Mr. Hayes could do to not only capture a percentage of that leakage but facilitate additional retail development within our community through the relationships he has developed with retail executives throughout his career.

Within a couple of weeks, I had the opportunity to hear Mr. Hayes speak to a large group of elected officials, community supporters, investors, college students and engaged citizens. It was there that I learned that Mr. Hayes had written a book entitled *City on a Hill: A Book on Cities and How to Make Them Better*. I immediately obtained a copy and read it within days. After all, if I was going to recommend hiring Mr. Hayes and his firm, Retail Attractions, to the City Council, I wanted to be as informed as possible on the tactics, philosophies and strategies Mr. Hayes was going to employ in our community.

City on a Hill offered much more than I expected. With nearly 20 years of local government experience, I could relate to and appreciated the real-life scenarios and examples used by Mr. Hayes. It quickly became apparent that throughout his career working in and consulting with local government entities, Mr. Hayes had maneuvered through and overcome many of the same obstacles and challenges that I continually faced as a City Manager. This included successfully partnering with and dealing with many of the same types of people that all of us encounter within our communities, from the optimistic community activist, willing to do whatever it takes to help the community succeed, to the C.A.V.E. person (Citizens Against Virtually Everything) bent on crushing any prospect of progress or change.

It suffices to say that Mr. Hayes exceeded our expectations. After hiring him and his firm, Retail Attractions, our community generated the highest annual sales tax revenues on record for multiple years and several retail and industrial business either opened new locations within our city or remodeled and expanded existing locations.

City on a Hill is a book for anyone who is involved in their community and wants to take that involvement to the next level. This includes City Managers, elected officials and engaged citizens who genuinely want to see their community not only succeed but thrive. Mr. Hayes' emphasis on relationships within communities and how those relationships directly and indirectly impact the overall health and viability of a local economy cannot be overstated. If you desire your community to be that "*City on a Hill* [that] cannot be hidden," this book should be step one.

Clayton Lucas has more than 18 years of local government experience and currently serves as a City Manager in his home state of Oklahoma. He is also the author of the best-selling novel, Iron Post Corner.